STEPPING OUT IN LOVE

Gayle Suzanne

Praise for *It's In The Little Things*

"Had to tell you, I'm already reading your book! I love it. Like a supportive, smart, fun conversation with your best girlfriend."

Leeza G

"From the very first page until the last, this book is amazing. It's funny, it's inspiring, it's a must-read book. Gayle Suzanne has nailed it with this book."

Mary C

"Gayle Suzanne stole my heart from the adorable little girl on the cover to the moment I burst out laughing. I was hooked and it was more a bursting forth from the heart for this simple book w/ its deep wisdom."

Susan R

"I never write reviews of books, but I needed to write this one. This book was inspirational for me. I was awed."

Lorraine C

"It's in the Little Things is sweet, uplifting, humorous and powerful. The messages are clear and concise teaching readers only how to focus on the little things in the quest for happiness and fulfillment."

Closed the Cover

"I have been a practicing psychologist for many years and I am still recommending this book to patients. Gayle truly captures the essence of life in an original and optimistic way. A strong standing ovation for Gayle; This is a timeless book!"

Teresa R

"As a man I found this not a fluffy chic book, but one that speaks to the soul. a great refresher on things we know but forget to live by in the hustle and bustle of life."

Tadd S

"Her writing style is relaxed and draws the reader in like you are sitting and having a cup of coffee (or wine) together. She gives anyone who has gone through traumatic events in their lives, whether it be abuse or bullying, a voice."

Sallie B

"Both my husband and I enjoyed 'It's In The Little Things." I also got a copy for a friend who is facing difficult times. I'm sure it will help her *and put a smile on her face!"*

Barbara N

"Gayle Suzanne reminds us to be our best self - regardless of the outcome in the moment."

Maureen W

"A smile shines through even dark times with practical suggestions which generate hope. Gayle's humor and practicality reward the reader with a down to earth, richly rewarding lifetime memories."

Jane L

"This book has helped me to understand that no matter what your situation is, you have a choice to be a victim or you can change your thinking and actions to become the victor. Gayle certainly demonstrates that in this collection of her life experiences."

Emmy M

"This book was one of the most enjoyable ones I had read in a long time. It opened my eyes on things I seemed to be stuck on, I also absolutely loved the format of short stories. I recommend this book to get entertained and to do some soul searching."

Roland P

"I found the book to be humorous, touching, and inspiring all at the same time. As a reader of the same age as the writer, the book resonated with me on many levels. There were times that I shed a tear while reading and other times when a loud belly laugh escaped. I would highly recommend this book and I plan to read it again and again and gift it to all my friends this year for their birthdays."

Angela R

"Although not preachy, Gayle Suzanne shares practical lessons that can help overcome feelings of self-doubt and inadequacy. She points out that simple acts of kindness towards others, such as a smile, can boost our own feelings of self-worth."

MaryEllen D

"Witty, charming, and appropriately self-deprecating, her breezy writing style and easy prose make this an eminently digestible book, even for those outside of her target demographic."

Tom S

STEPPING OUT IN LOVE

Gayle Suzanne

Copyright @ 2018 Gayle Suzanne

Gayle Suzanne, CPC, ALB, ELI-MP
Certified Professional Coach, Author, Motivational Speaker, TV Host
and Producer
Charlton, MA 01507
Gayle@gaylesuzanne.com

Visit her website at www.gaylesuzanne.com
YouTube: Moving Forward with Gayle Suzanne

For all who have gone through a painful breakup,

There is hope for a magnificent future.

Dedication

I am blessed to have many compassionate, generous and spirited people in my life.

Life is all about connections, experiences and shared memories. It's about family, friends, and acquaintances who might do one tiny thing that changes your life. It's about people who come into your life for a fleeting time to teach you that crucial lesson, or those who enter your life and never leave, because your connection is deep and meaningful. It's about lifting each other up and allowing yourself to be lifted up. It's about that person who gently picks you off that hamster wheel and points you in a better direction. It's about honesty, laughter, loyalty, silliness, grief, acceptance, challenges, triumphs and joy. I am fortunate to have lived through these experiences, and then some, with those I love and cherish.

I dedicate this book to them.

Heartfelt thanks to:

John. Our relationship is living proof that people can happily move on after a divorce. You are stable, solid, and true. I love our life together. I count my blessings every day.

Nick, Becca and Dan. I'm so proud of you! Merging our families has been an amazing blessing and learning experience. You have enriched my life so much!

Heather, Becca and Chris F. Your keen eyes, honesty and thoughtful comments have helped craft this final product. Always grateful! This book would never have come together without you.

Dr. Teresa R and Jim B for your amazing insight. You encouraged me to take risks and in the process I became more confident and self-assured. You both helped me through critical times with your steadfast support, wisdom, guidance and compassion.

Special shout out to friends and family who made me laugh, told it to me straight, talked me down at 2 am, watched me blubber cry, reached out to see how I was doing, inspired me and gave me great material for this this book, brought me cough drops when I was sick, babysat and cherished Becca, partied with me after work, listened to me for countless hours, welcomed me into their families with open arms, invited me to dinner, vacationed with me, and simply loved me!! Angela C, Angela R, Anthony, Becca N, Candace, Cappy, Carol, Chris D, Chris L, Chris G, Chris M, Cindy, Courtaney, Courtney, Darlene, Deb F, Deb G, Deb K, Diane, Dolores, Donna, Frank D, Frank G, Gary, Greg, Harry, Heather C, Heather F, Heather K, Irene, Jack, Jan, Jane, Jayme, Jim, John H, John M, Kara, Karen L, Karen M, Keith, Kelli, Kellie, Kelly, Kris, Leah, Linda M, Lisa L, Lori, Lorraine C, Luanne, Marcia, Mark, Maryellen, MaryJane, Maura, Melody, Melon, Pat, Patty, Rea, Rhonda, Robin, Roland, Ronnie, Stephanie, Steve, Sue R, Susan S, Tama, Tara, Toni, Valerie, Vanessa, Vicki

Book cover and design by:
Victoria Boucher – victoriaboucherphotography.com
Jack Nichols - jcknichols.com

Preface

If someone told me twenty years ago I would be living a fulfilling, passionate life surrounded by loving family and friends I would have thought they were cracking up or smoking crack. The beginning of my life was rough and after dealing with a painful divorce I thought I would break. I felt damaged and worthless. I decided to take time to dig deep and learn lessons from obstacles I had faced.

After my divorce, self-care was my number one goal. I spent time uncovering my true, authentic self that had been covered up with insecurities, berating self-talk, overly harsh self-judgment and people pleasing. As I grew more confident, my close inner circle was filled with supportive, genuine people who helped me believe in myself. I detached from any negative, toxic influences and began stepping out and experiencing exciting new adventures, proving I can live a wonderfully spirited life on my own.

Once I was completely open and ready to move on, John came into my life. We dated and eventually married and merged our families together. The purpose of this book is to offer hope to anyone going through a difficult breakup. Tips and suggestions are shared to encourage you to step out of your comfort zone and change your perspective on divorce, being single, dating and merging a stepfamily. *Stepping Out in Love* is written from a woman's point of view, but certainly suitable for male readers as well!

The cover of the book represents the joys in my life. The sunflowers symbolize our family – John and I are the larger sunflowers and the 3 smaller ones represent our 3 children, Nick, Becca and Dan. Sunflowers, with their vibrant colors signify happiness, sturdiness, beauty and strength. Blowing bubbles is one of my simple pleasures. They are fun, inexpensive and playful. Sunflowers and bubbles are two of my favorite things… and so is my cherished family.

Table of Contents

Part 1

AFTER THE BREAKUP

NOW WHAT AM I SUPPOSED TO DO?

Once the judge slammed down his gavel and flatly stated "Divorce granted", Room D became frighteningly silent. I thought at a bare minimum a band would burst into play and confetti would pour down from the ceiling. But instead, the awkward moment after the slam seemed to last an eternity. The whole court thing was totally anticlimactic. I stared straight ahead as my lawyer clasped his briefcase shut. I'm sure his thoughts shifted to his next client where the wife was putting up a fight for the electric turkey carver and the timeshare in the sticks. I thanked him and watched him disappear around the corner. This man, who months ago was a total stranger, morphed into a trusted confidante, a repeated witness to my ugly cry, and a champion and cheerleader for my future. Fast forward thirty seconds, I'm standing in the hallway with my now newly-titled ex-husband. We hugged goodbye, wished each other luck and turned in opposite directions. Ironically, the same way our futures would go.

I took a few deep breaths and walked outside. I could not muster up the courage to go back to work even though I was within a five-minute walk to my luxurious 3x4 cubicle. I found a quiet spot on the grass behind the courthouse and plopped myself down. Although I was next to a busy street, it was as if the world went silent. I felt so alone in that moment. Virtually numb. With my back leaning up against an enormous oak tree, I lit a cigarette, smelled the scent of freshly cut grass, shut my eyes, exhaled and tried to imagine what my future would look like. Even though we had been separated for several months, this was the final nail in the coffin. No turning back now.

Taking my wedding vows before God was something I took seriously. Even though I tried my best, I wondered what I could have done differently or how I contributed to the demise of our marriage. I started to weep, not a gut-wrenching cry, but more like a whimpering baby who wanted to be held. If only I could swaddle myself in the leaves of this big ole oak tree. I did not allow myself to open the flood gates as I intended to return to work. If I took the afternoon off I would just have been a basket case, so I walked back to my wonderful co-workers and went on a search for cake. There's always cake.

Having grown up with divorced parents, breaking up with my husband was something I did everything in my power to avoid. For my 4-year old daughter, Becca, my wish for her was to feel secure, adored and to be living under the same roof as both mommy and daddy. For me, I did not want to start over. I did not want to mess up her life. I did not want to live alone and have the mailman discover me lying on my kitchen being nibbled on by my kitties. I did not want the pain in my heart. I did not want my daughter to end up on a street corner.

But sometimes both parties can do everything in their power to make a marriage work, and it simply cannot be salvaged. I was in shock at first, and over time progressed through each of the grieving stages. Denial, anger, guilt, depression, acceptance. I invented some other grieving stages along the way, but they did not have an official name...such as the I-hate-mowing-the (f-word) lawn-and-having-pebbles-smack-me-in-the-face phase.

Being a 34-year old woman who was independent and strong, it was foreign to me to start asking for support and encouragement. I was constantly seeking out anyone who would assure me that all would be okay, even if was said by someone sliding off a bar stool. I sought guidance from those who had been divorced and were thriving. I had to create my life over again. A day at a time. Sometimes one minute at a time.

WHERE DID I GO?

When I walked down the aisle in my early twenties, I was thankful to finally have found a partner who would fix my problems, restore the emotionally damaged younger me, consistently lift my spirits, repeatedly tell me how amazing I was and love me for me, even though my own love tank was running on empty.

I never understood what losing myself meant until I lost myself and had to figure out where I went. I would hear the term in a movie but never fully grasped the concept. What I eventually discovered was that losing myself meant constantly living in fear – fear of rejection, fear of saying the wrong thing, fear of revealing my damaged worthless self, fear of not being good enough and fear of not being loved. Being in so much fear that I did everything in my power to do the *right* thing to be loved. In the process, my true essence chipped and slipped away.

As I began reflecting on certain behaviors in the marriage, I had to take responsibility for the unrealistic expectation of wanting my ex-husband to complete me. Jerry McGuire might have been able to complete Dorothy Boyd, but in reality, no one can complete someone else, no matter how charismatic, rich or confident they are. It was not my ex-husband's role to fix me. As I figured out later (through deep thoughts, years lying horizontal on the shrink couch and countless Adult Children of Alcoholics meetings) such lofty expectations took the accountability off of me and onto him.

It is now when I must reflect on my past to figure out how I got here. The beginning of my life was rough. My mother struggled with alcohol, which caused me to live in a daily state of uncertainty and fear. Each day, I never knew what to expect. Most of the time she was angry, manipulative and controlling. She suffered from a disease, but because I was a young child, I lacked the understanding that she was sick and addicted. All I knew was I did not feel worthy of love and no matter what I did, I could not please her.

I was bullied by other kids since before first grade and the harassment continued through middle school. Throw in a sexual abuse situation by a trusted adult and I win the reject award. I survived three decades feeling unsafe, full of worry, shame, guilt, and co-dependent.

Thankfully my parents enrolled me in a private high school to remove me from my daily torment. This ridiculed, shame-based, chubby 13-year old was blessed with a fresh start. As I began this new life, I befriended jocks, brains, druggies, shy kids and class clowns. I perfected a chameleon persona and finally had a super-duper eclectic group of friends.

Looking back, this was the initial stage of the real Gayle slipping away and being replaced by the Gayle who morphed into whomever anyone wanted her to be. You see, I wanted to be accepted so badly I would do and say anything to be liked. I began to lose sight of who I was and what I wanted. If someone liked blue, I liked blue. If they were sad, I was sad. If they said jump, I'd say, "How high?" after I made them a sandwich.

I intuitively knew that people hung out with me because they sensed I could be easily swayed or manipulated. I was obsessed with keeping the peace, even to the point of accepting unacceptable behavior and apologizing for things I had no part in. Terrified of confrontation, living with no boundaries, feeling responsible for other's actions - these insecurities and fears placed a thick film over the real me.

The Gayle that God created had lost her true essence and authenticity. Time to get that essence back! The how is scattered over the following pages. Stay tuned…

DYNAMICS CHANGE

Divorce is not only about two people living separately, it's about learning how to live all over again.

There's a major difference when you become single after a long-term relationship than when you are single in your early years. When you are a young adult, your single lifestyle is generally carefree. The world is at your feet. Potential suitors are everywhere! Chances are you have a group of single friends and are quite possibly living with one or two of them. If your roommate has a date on Saturday night, you have the option of calling other singles to chill with. Male, female, it didn't matter; just a bunch of friends together. You have the Saturday night friend nights where you make spaghetti dinner together and watch movies. When I was in my early 20's I had a boyfriend, but never had a shortage of single friends to be with at a moment's notice when he had other plans.

Once you split up and suddenly find yourself single again, life doesn't return to the way it was. It's a whole different ball game, cupcake. Now when you are planning Saturday night friend spaghetti night, you might not have as many options. Several friends have kids and want to stay home. Another couple would prefer caviar and champagne rather than canned sauce and boxed angel hair. The straggler single friends that remain on your list usually leave the house to go out when you are ready for bed.

Below are several issues I had to deal with after the split:

- Finding the appropriate person to select as an emergency contact. My daughter would be the obvious choice, but she was only four and couldn't read or write, so I had to pick someone who could at least count past ten.

- Attending a wedding without a date. You are seated at the singles' table next to Ernie, who is wearing white gym socks and has an exposed butt crack; desperate Sheila whose nipples are showing through her white dress; and bourbon-breathed Bob who is staring at Sheila. The only person who asks you to dance is cousin Buster, who is 62 years old, lives with his Mee-maw and has cracker crumbs in his beard.
- Getting used to sitting in the backseat when you carpool with your married friends. I spent 5 years patiently waiting to be freed from the childproofed back door.
- Dealing with the fact that some of your "friends" will no longer be available because they 'sided' with your ex.
- Filling out five billion forms to change your last name.
- Adapting to living alone. It can be depressing and lonely. When you are alone in the house while married to a mate who has gone out to run errands, you might jump for joy that you have a chunk of time for yourself, but when you're alone, you're alone.
- Accepting the loss of material possessions you once owned. Your ex might have received custody of your favorite recliner or the turkey fryer. Or maybe he took ownership of something a bit unorthodox, like, um, the adult toys you used together. (yeah, that's true…beware if a new guy gives you an erotic present with a broken seal.)
- Becoming accustomed to house creaky sounds in the middle of the night. This can be quite startling, especially after watching The Blair Witch Project. I checked under the bed and in the closet for months afterward.
- Finding a new group of single friends to hang with. This might stretch you because you might have to meet new single friends.
- Relying on yourself to take care of meals, laundry, car repairs, rides to sporting events, disciplining children, doctor appointments, grocery shopping, parent conferences, class projects, ironing, attending recitals and practice, clothes shopping, cleaning, dusting, vacuuming, changing sheets,

holiday get togethers, mailing cards, kissing boo boos, buying stamps, changing the Brita filter, emptying and filling the dishwasher, washing windows, steam cleaning floors, salting the walkway, taking out the garbage, properly filling recycle bins, watching Lifetime movies, preparing tax information, making Mickey Mouse pancakes, mailing birthday cards, wrapping presents, paying the bills, weeding, waiting for the four hour window for plumbers, electricians, cable guys, and appliance repair workers, brushing and flossing, reading bedtime stories, going to post office, feeding the birds and hummingbirds, snowplowing, replacing lightbulbs, giving tubbies, sewing buttons on coats, shopping for entire family for Christmas, trimming shrubs, throwing out leftovers, baking cupcakes for PTA events, cleaning gutters, going to the bank, cleaning kitty litter boxes, disposing of spiders found on your child's bedroom wall, sewing Halloween costumes, attending dance recitals and show choirs, oiling squeaky hinges, playing Candy Land and Don't Break The Ice, dry cleaning clothes, picking up prescriptions, coloring my hair, unclogging toilets, fixing leaky faucets, ironing, staining the deck, touch up painting, folding laundry, making school lunches, sweeping the porch, hugging and kissing the children, cleaning the garage, filling windshield washer fluid, trimming the shrubs, removing caterpillars from the front deck, removing hair from the drain, cleaning clutter, going to work, taking care of yourself and children when ill, feeding and watering pets, take care of their bathroom habits, stocking toilet paper at all times, changing lightbulbs, helping with homework, planning birthday parties, replacing the battery in the beeping smoke detectors, learning how to shut off the damn TV that requires 40 remotes.

Be patient with yourself. Change is all around you, but you can do this!

JUDGE THEE NOT

I did not want to be divorced. I did not want to be a divorced woman in her 30's. I did not want to be a divorced woman in her 30's with a young child. I did not want to be a divorced woman in her 30's with a young child starting to date again. I did not want to be a fox in a box in a house with a mouse.

I had to eventually accept the truth that I was, in fact, a divorced woman. The stereotypical woman who could not keep her man. A failure. I could not help but think that when I went out in public, people saw a red-letter D carved into my forehead. To be honest, I would have preferred they thought it stood for Dummy or Dufus. To get past this morphed imagery, I had to reverse my negative perception of a divorced person, because I was now one.

My preconceived judgement was that there was something wrong with a person who was divorced. Someone *must* have caused the breakdown, someone had to be 100% at fault. Furthermore, I'd be cautious around the person I labeled as the one who destroyed the family – goodness knows I did not want the divorce disease to rub off on me.

Admittedly, I was ignorant.

So, there I stood, alone. Now one of *them*.

I was acutely aware of the water cooler talk. The speculation, whispering, the perceived looks of disappointment, biased opinions, comments behind my back.

"If I was her, I would have left sooner." "I would have sucked it up." "I would have not been such a nag."

I knew these conversations so well because I did the same thing to others!

But my reality was that I did my absolute best to save the marriage. I tried everything I could think of to make it work. I made mistakes for sure, but I put my best foot forward. The decisions I made were the best I could make at the time.

People split up for a variety of reasons. Sometimes one goes this a-way, the other goes that a-way. They grow apart, the pressures of life might be too heavy, sometimes they are simply not meant to be together. People evolve and if they do not grow together, they grow distant. The bottom line is that at least one party in the marriage is not happy. That feeling might result in certain behaviors such as indifference, grumpiness, excessive drinking or drug use, infidelity, gambling, overspending, overeating, staying out late with friends. There are a million symptoms which result from irreconcilable differences. I believe these behaviors are symptoms of a deeper root of unhappiness.

I do believe in my heart that people enter marriage with the best of intentions and have every desire to make their union a success. Unfortunately, sometimes it doesn't. Over time, things happen. It's life. It might not be fair, it might not be what we expected, but love brought two people together in the first place. If we can remember that, it helps shift our perspective.

I need to remind myself that it is not my business to judge what happened in another person's relationship. We are all human and while some behaviors are more blatant than others, I do not live their lives, so I will make my best attempt to refrain from judgement.

IT'S MY SHOWER AND I'LL CRY IF I WANT TO

For months, it seemed like all I did was bawl my eyes out. I should have bought stock in tissues. I could have cried my way all the way to the bank. Cha-ching.

The bathroom was cry-time place for me. I estimate that I drew close to 3,098,382,717 baths the months following my divorce. Something about the hot water, exfoliating lotion and sea salts put me in a tranquil state where I became vulnerable enough to release my pain. I would shut the lights, fire up a few scented candles, put on a soothing CD, hop in the steaming tub and place a scorching facecloth over my face. The hot water on my skin seemed to have the power to break the walls all the way down to my soul.

I would hum, whimper, meditate and pray. It was solitude time to unwind, soothe my anxious state of mind and heal my broken spirit.

Often when showering, I would stand underneath the hot water with my head down, hair falling in front of my face and just wail. It was as if my tears and the running water together cleansed both the inside and outside of my body. At times I found myself curled up in the fetal position on the tub floor. My cries resembled that of a howling animal. Those were the moments when the pain of deep hurts surfaced and consumed my mind; the heartache of not experiencing my mother's affection and acceptance, the anguish of memories of kids ridiculing me and excluding me, the sadness when girls whispered and laughed at me behind my back, the rejection of boys avoiding me as if I was a disease. And now, add a failed marriage to the list.

These were the times I felt so hopeless I had no choice but to completely surrender to God. My hurt was so raw. This was when I knew I had no control over my future, I could not do anything about my past and I had to let go and give my life over to God. Give it up to Him because I could not handle the intense sorrow. After I mustered up the strength to stand upright, I felt a huge weight lifted off my shoulders. Thankfully, my thoughts transitioned to a peaceful state and an instinctual knowing that God would take care of me. Somehow.

Tears heal. It is critical to release painful feelings. Getting out all my emotions helped me more than I can convey. I became less harsh on myself and realized that most situations I endured were not my fault. I accepted the notion that I was not junk. I learned to be tender with myself. I began to ease up on myself during painful moments.

As time went on, two days would pass by without a tear. I acknowledged that I was on my way to restoring my life. I had given myself permission to cry, to get mad, to eat Cocoa Puffs for dinner, to feel upset, to vent. I also promised myself to be tender and kind, and under no circumstance would I be mean to myself during these vulnerable times. Crying is not weakness, it is a healthy way to deal with pain.

Cry. It's okay. Let it out. It's good to release and surrender.

Too bad crying is not a cardio activity. If it was, I'd be *oh so* skinny!

FEAR OF ABANDONMENT

This is a biggie for me. Ever since I was a wee one, as far back as age four, I feared my parents would leave me. Ma had a problem with alcohol and was volatile. I rarely felt safe in my own home. That fear was most present when I was separated from my parents lying alone in my big girl bed at night. Every stinkin' night after the lights went out, I would get up and tiptoe down the hall, through the kitchen, peek around the corner into the living room and look for daddy's slippers at the end of his recliner. If I saw his feet, I breathed a sigh of relief and returned to bed. Every night I walked that same walk, some nights I would make the trip as many as five times. Each time he was there. I never wanted him to leave us. This nightly ritual went on for years. Once I was fully satisfied with my slipper checks, I would ultimately end up in my big sister Chris' bed. Sleeping next to her made me feel safe. She was my protector, a role I unintentionally placed on her throughout my young life.

Daddy loved his family, but since my mother could be unpredictable, I sensed early on that being physically abandoned could be a real possibility. After one of their horrible fights, Ma asked Chris and me to help her slide a big wooden piece of furniture in front of the front door, so Daddy could not get back in the house. The last thing we wanted to do was lock him out, but we were small children and did what we were told. After the blockade was in place, I went over to the window and watched him walk further and further away from the house. My panic and fear intensified with each step. On that dreadful day, my little four-year old self used all her might, opened the living room window and screamed at the top of my lungs for him to stay. I adored my Daddy and knew he would not leave us, yet that day planted a seed that he could be kept from us. That was a terrifying night for me.

He never left. Ever.

A few years later when I was in first grade, Chris and I were dropped off at our elementary school for Saturday morning CCD class. Once class was over, Ma or Daddy would pick us up. On this random Saturday, we walked out to the parking lot and no one was waiting for us. Our big Oldsmobile Regency that comfortably fit 9 people in the front seat and got 6 miles per gallon was not there. As the minutes slowly ticked by, I watched all the other kids hop in their family cars and drive away. Panic began to bubble up in me. At first, just normal panic. But as soon as we were the only two children left on the school property, I went into full-blown, crazy nutzo maniac panic. Pushing through the double doors, running back into the school and down the hall shrieking (as if Freddy Krueger and his razor blades were chasing me) arms flailing, hyperventilating. I bet the custodian was looking around for Freddy also. What else would make a little kid freak out like that?

Even today, I clearly remember thinking "This is it. They left us, I knew it would happen!" My sister, who was not a cry baby like me, tried to calm me down. She was the older, more mature and wiser of the two of us, but there was no soothing this freaked out precious fat-faced kid. I was hysterical and basically inconsolable. Finally, daddy pulled in the parking lot.

Daddy! Our Daddy! Daddy's here! Thank God Daddy's here!

Deep breath and sigh of relief.

He apologized as I was sniveling, wiping my wet nose on my sleeve, and trying to calm my breath in the backseat. He didn't leave us. He simply lost track of time. He didn't abandon us. He was just late.

I think back to that emotional morning and wondered if Chris was scared too. If she was, she did not let on. She was protecting me once again. I am beyond grateful for my big sister. I wonder if she put her fear aside so that she could comfort me. I think she did. That's amazing because she was only nine years old and a member of the same dysfunctional,

33

violent household as me. There must have been some feeling of angst, yet she remained chill, and I believe it was for my benefit. Goodness knows, if she lost it too, I probably would have jumped in the front seat of the next car that passed by – completely ignoring the stranger danger rule.

Fast forward 30 years later. Becca is in first grade. My schedule allowed me to leave work early on Thursdays, so I could pick her up at the bus stop. One random Thursday I had a conference call that ran over its scheduled time. Apparently, I had a temporary brain freeze and forgot I had to pick her up right after the call. I was late - an hour late to be exact. Mother of the Year award recipient here. I drove 95 miles an hour on two wheels to arrive home quickly. I ran into the house and listened to a voicemail from the school saying Becca was safe. The bus driver would drop her off at home when he finished dropping off all the other children on his route.

As the bus pulled in front of the house, I darted outside and repeatedly expressed my gratitude and sincere apology to the driver. "Thank you for taking care of Becca! It won't happen again!" I assured him.

Becca stepped off the bus with her big brown Hershey kiss eyes and looked up at me with a goofy grin on her face, dry eyed. "Gee mom, what happened to you?" No tears. No panic. Instead, I got the impression she thought it was a special treat because she got to sit up front with the driver.

Instant flashback to my panic filled CCD Saturday.

I asked her, "Honey, were you nervous I wasn't going to come get you?" In my head I thought, 'Honey, were you emotionally scarred for life? Did you go screaming up and down the bus aisle? Did you run from Freddy and his razor blade fingers?'

"Nope. I just thought you forgot Mom." She skipped off to her room and started to play with her Barbies. Not a care in the world. I brought her a snack and she was dressing Barbie in her pink stilettos as if nothing had happened.

We were both 6 years old. In a comparable situation, I was scared, unsafe and felt my family would leave me. She was secure, confident with the expectation and knowing that I would be there for her.

I thought about this for hours. How could our reactions be so different? My upbringing with an alcoholic mother made me feel unsafe and not secure, because the environment I grew up in was not consistent and stable. It was volatile, erratic and unpredictable.

This was a proud mamma moment for me. This was a sign that I was breaking the fear of abandonment cycle.

So, on to my romantic encounters. Go make a pot of coffee, this is going to take a while.

This is my take on how not dealing with my abandonment issues showed up in my potential relationships. Since I never healed the abandonment fear I had as a child, I carried those insecurities with me as an adult. Not dealing with my issues manifested into a deep-down feeling that everyone would leave me. They would throw me away. Just like a piece of trash. I made every attempt to 'keep' someone in a relationship with me. Basically, I ignored my needs and became the all-accommodating partner. That meant continuing to say yes when I wanted to say no, apologizing for things I had no part in, putting others needs before my own, maintaining an irrational fear of other's anger, and living with constant anxiety that I would do something wrong. In a nutshell, I did everything in my power to not be abandoned. This yummy behavior, by the way, showed up in all sorts of relationships – authority figures, friendships, romantic, coworkers, bosses.

And guess what? It worked for a while. Hell, who wouldn't jump at the

35

chance to be with someone who would roll over and play dead if asked to? The giving in, apologizing and conformity kept things peaceful and content. But eventually I became angry, resentful, bitter and depressed. Because I was so busy pleasing the world, my needs were not getting met. My anger and resentment came out in fits of screaming rage, then guilt, then depression. The pattern of my destructive behavior went like this: I would hit the end of my very long rope, aggressively stand up for myself, usually cursing and yelling, then feel bad that I lost my temper, apologize for it, then become hopeless and despondent because nothing had changed.

My fear of abandonment also showed up by pushing people away before they pushed me away. I could never fully let my guard down, because as soon as I did, the target was on my back. So, if I sabotaged the relationship by being irrational or a jerk, then they would leave me.

See, I knew they would leave me!

What I did not realize was that in the midst of protecting myself from being abandoned by others, I abandoned myself. Others may have rejected me, and I followed suit. My feelings, needs, desires, wants, dreams, and passions were unconsciously buried, all the way down to China.

Because I finally came to this amazing understanding, which hit me like a wrecking ball, I now have an opportunity to reclaim my abandoned self and nurture, hug, snug and accept her with open arms. Without blame or self-destructive thoughts, I was committed and willing to give myself the tenderness and compassion I so deeply craved.

As a single woman, I recognized that I can get in tune with my emotions and feelings and offer myself the care I deserve. I can be quiet when needed. I can dance around and act silly when I want to. I can develop an intuition that is so laser focused there is no doubt which actions will serve my highest good.

I am a true believer that once an awareness rears its prickly, uncomfortable, unsettling, ugly head, that is our opportunity to jump on the self-help train and become willing to learn the critical lessons we are supposed to learn.

This recognition will probably sting like a bunch of hornets, but you cannot do anything about behavior until you become aware of it. Once you are aware, then you can tweak behavior and move forward.

I am identifying tools to nurture and care for myself. Finding my voice, setting limits, detaching, communicating, addressing my needs, making discerning decisions, opening myself up to diverse types of love, trusting my instincts, eating greens, flossing, meditation, gifting myself, and surrounding myself with positive influences are all part of becoming the woman I was meant to be.

It is certainly not an overnight fix, yet I am committed to developing an allegiance to myself that is so strong I will never abandon myself again, even if I am alone forever.

BODY DEAREST

Being underweight is an issue I never had to deal with. Sweets, gooey cookies and chocolate are like oxygen to me. I need them to live. Although overweight, I am still able to climb a set of three stairs and make it through fifteen minutes of a Zumba class. Kidding aside, losing weight after my divorce was not at the forefront of my mind. I had gone through a depression after the split. Not debilitating, but enough to keep my mind occupied with other issues that did not include my squishy parts.

Stress affects people in many ways. For me, stress messes with my belly. When panic rears its beastly head, I gag and then vomit. Not sure why I wasn't blessed with a graceful stress reaction, like clearer skin or a higher metabolism, but those are the cards I was dealt. Luckily, over time, I have learned to control myself and only gag. As a result, after the split, even though I consciously followed the food pyramid each day, I lost quite a bit of weight.

At the same time, my dear friend and coworker was going through a divorce also. Her physical stress release was shaking. Probably once a day while in the thick of our divorce dramas, we would pop into a vacant office and confide in each other about the day's emotional trauma. She would be shaking, I would be gagging. The funny thing, and it was hysterical to us, was that we just accepted each other as we were. We understood. We got it. We knew the pain in our hearts transformed into physical symptoms. We must have looked ridiculous to those who glanced our way as they walked by to make a photocopy, but for us, it was a special bonding experience between two gagging, shaking chicks who just wanted to make it through the day.

No matter what the exterior looks like, the interior will break through. I slimmed down quite a bit. In due time I fit into the boots I wore in high school. My triple chins downsized to double. My Buddha belly shrunk a few sizes. I wore tight short skirts with high heels. I strutted now. Feeling empowered on the outside I began getting quite a bit of attention from men, several of whom were married. I was friendly but hooking up with a married man was not a possibility, no matter how horrible he told me his wife was.

Even though my outsides looked pretty dang spiffy, my insides had not caught up yet. As discussed in previous chapters, I had a lot of inner crap to scrape out and clean up. My head was messed up and there were rotten layers of stinky, stanky onions inside of me. It was time to bid adieu to the guilt, the shame, the blaming, the self-sabotaging, the complaining, the impatience, the self-loathing, the victim mentality. I was preparing to toss it all overboard.

It was time to retrain my brain and create a healthier future. Even though I desperately yearned to be in a relationship, I knew that I knew that I knew I would end up in the same type of situation if I did not take this alone time to work on myself. I intuitively knew that doing the same thing repeatedly would produce the same result. That little voice in my belly knew that cleaning out my gunk was the only feasible option for me to become healthy in my mind and spirit and to eventually be a healthy partner.

Kind of like an enema for my brain.

PEEL THOSE LAYERS OFF

When you split up with a partner you have been with for years, a common feeling is to want to sprint into another relationship. This guy will make me happy! This one will change my life! He is the one who will turn my life around!

This may not be the best answer. For me, it most definitely was not the right choice, no matter how many times I tried to convince myself otherwise.

I needed to work through my own stuff before even considering getting involved with another man. My lack of confidence, trust issues, co-dependency, and panic about the future had to be addressed. Part of me (the left part, in case you're wondering) wanted to jump road-runner style into another marriage so I did not have to deal with my crap, yet the other, slightly wiser, right part of me fully understood I needed to spend quality time pressing through the self-sabotaging behaviors that made me a train wreck.

While attempting to heal, I was terrified to "go there" and address my true feelings. I convinced myself that if I felt the feelings of the agonizing memories of my past, I would literally explode.

Splat.

I had perfected the art of dealing with mild misconduct of others, but when it came to my dark, shameful, deep-rooted behavior and past, I'd rather pluck my eyeballs out with a skewer and pretend it never happened. But I had to face my truth head on and deal with it once and for all. Realistically I knew, after researching on Google, that no one ever splatted after dealing with painful events. There goes *that* excuse.

Is it enjoyable? Uh, No. Is it necessary? Yes. Yes. Yes.

Why is it necessary? Why can't I just bundle up my hurts and woes, put them in a shoebox and toss them in the garbage?

When we do not deal with emotional hurts, similar situations will appear until we learn the lesson life is trying to teach us.

I had to take a deep breath and look at myself in an honest way to heal my broken self. I needed to find my true essence. I had oodles of noodles of work to do. The following nuggets guided me toward a better life:

<u>Stop Re-living Past Hurts.</u>

Yes, you were abused as a child. Yes, you were in an abusive marriage. Yes, you have been hurt. Yes, you have gone through sad, traumatic times. Yes, it was not fair.

Each time we relive a painful event repeatedly, we are focusing our energy and thoughts on the sadness and pain of that situation. I remember thinking about a traumatic incident that happened in 1987, and the scene was repeated over and over in my mind. Thinking this way cemented the fact that I was not good enough. That type of thinking was not in my best interest if I wanted to press past my past.

Acknowledge your hurt. Write in your journal. Yes, you were abused. You did not deserve that. Yes, you have been undeniably hurt and endured horrible situations. You did not deserve that. It was not your fault. Acknowledge that. This is a critical and necessary step to heal. Eventually there will be a time when you must let go so you can be open to the future blessings life has in store for you. I do not believe we will live our best future until we release the pains of the past. Because we will carry that pain, hurt, victim mentality and resentment with us into new situations and relationships.

If you constantly look at the pain of the past and dwell there, it will be hard for you to improve your situation. If your thoughts are consumed in this dark and dreadful place, you might tell yourself that nothing good will ever happen and your future will be bleak. I thought this way for years and it kept me stuck. I will never love again because I was hurt. They will all hurt me. My life will suck forever. One big suck-fest.

The thing is you are not the same person you were years ago. You are not the same person you were yesterday. You have the present time to grow, pamper and nurture yourself, trust your intuition and protect yourself from harmful situations. You are wiser and more experienced. You understand that not every person will hurt you. You have the discernment to develop a bond with someone who will treat you right.

You have the capability, wisdom, power and smarts to make choices that serve your highest good.

Stop Blaming.

Oh, blaming your ex is beyond easy to do! You will tell anyone who will listen, even if they are unconscious. Your morphed image of yourself as a perfect partner is exaggerated. I replayed how many balanced meals I put on the table dressed in my ball gown and pearls, how my personality lit up every room I walked into, and how my princess like and ultra-pleasant demeanor made up for the fact that I was needy and insecure.

Blaming the other person can somehow justify our own behavior. It seemed like all I did was go over the same stuff repeatedly. Talking about my sad divorce, the stress of being a single parent, and my lonely life became my identity. My free-spirited, adventurous, lighthearted personality transformed each time I repeated a "poor me" story. I had *me* on my mind all the time. After a while, I got the sense that my whining was starting to wear on those around me. That was a subtle clue to smarten up and be grateful for the new life I was creating. It was a wake up call for me to plan my future rather than obsess about my past.

We can come up with Houdini-like moves to slither away from taking responsibility for our actions, even if we convince ourselves we did not contribute to the brokenness of the marriage. When we blame the other person, we take the focus off ourselves.

It takes two to tango. One person's actions could have been more harmful, blatant and obvious, but each person played a role in the demise. Moving forward, we can only change ourselves.

I am not suggesting that what you went through was not difficult, unfair or brutal, but sometimes we get stuck and stay in that sad place much longer than the pain's expiration date. Sometimes we rent space there for years. We get so angry or depressed that we constantly re-live those awful memories. I know, I've been there. But at some point, if you want to move on, once the tears have fallen and you've vented and screamed into a pillow a million times, releasing the pain will be a healing step. There is so much life out there, and when you continually find fault and blame someone else, it takes you away from the present and the mind-blowing things that are in store for you, right at this moment!

At some point, I had to draw line in the sand, move from victim to owning it. This action set me on my path to freedom.

Revisit the Past for Growth.

Even though I just suggested that you not dwell on the past (I'm a woman, I can change my mind), it is crucial to *revisit* the past to learn from our decisions, reactions, passive aggressive and self-sabotaging behaviors, and choices we've made while in the relationship. By getting in touch with why we reacted the way we did, we can alter our behavior in the future. I went to counseling twice a week for a long time, trying to figure out how to be a better person, make more productive decisions and not repeat my past missteps. And most importantly, to give myself validation.

During this introspective period, I acknowledged that I was volatile when I didn't get my way. I would go from zero to 100 in a second, like a toddler. I would verbally lash out and bring up unresolved issues that had nothing to do with the issue we were discussing. I imagined I acted this way because I stuffed my feelings. When an opportunity presented itself to let it all out, I let more than all of it out, and not in a pleasant way.

Now that I realize there is a more productive way to handle a confrontation, when an issue comes up I will attempt to talk about it when it arises, rather than stuffing and exploding. I have learned to count to ten or take a few deep breaths and try to be calm and patient to discuss conflict in an adult way. I will listen and fully comprehend what he has to say, rather than waiting for him to stop so I can yell my point. I will fair fight. This type of looking back is beneficial and constructive. My current husband thanks me for this!

Parts of ourselves die as we spiritually evolve. When we release our behaviors that no longer work, it is creating space for something better. This can be a painful process, but the pain is temporary. Don't hold onto to the old, invite and embrace the new. New, sound behaviors will only enhance your entire life!

It dawned on me that sometimes people make mistakes and that because I was on the receiving end of their anger and frustration, it didn't mean I was the *cause* of the mistake.

Another huge awareness was that I am highly triggered when I am not heard. If I am dismissed or ignored by anyone, especially someone in a position of authority, I instantly become agitated and visibly upset. Instead of letting a silent rage fester in me, I can now confront the person in a firm, calm manner and let my voice be heard. This adjustment has made an enormous impact on me.

Revisiting past behaviors is not an exercise to beat up on yourself. It is quite the opposite. It is taking a look at how your behaviors might have contributed to a lack of communication, how not using your voice allowed you to go without, how stuffing and shutting down of your own feelings lead to a shutting down of the relationship. These visits to the past are so personal for everyone, but critical for our growth.

Create your Childhood Now, as an Adult.

Some of us did not grow up with a carefree childhood. When I was 6-years old, my mother bought me an alarm clock for my birthday. This gift, she explained, meant that since I was a big girl it was now time for me to wake myself up each morning and get myself ready for school. So, starting in first grade I would set my shiny new alarm clock, get up, brush my teeth, get dressed, eat a pop tart and walk to the bus stop. I would see my mother when I came home from school. As I got older many days she did not make dinner so my sister Chris, at the ripe old age of 10 or 11, began preparing dinner so Daddy would have something to eat when he came home from work.

As a result, a carefree, whimsical childhood passed us by and was replaced by heavy duty responsibilities at way too young of an age.

I can now choose to create my own childhood. I still have a responsibility to pay the bills and take care of the kids, but I can also play Nintendo, act life a goofball, skip down the street and make snow angels. It's never too late to savor life like a small child. I think it is necessary to reward yourself with silliness and craziness. I have found real innocence and joy in my life. And I believe my childlike nature is one of my most appealing qualities. Weeeeeeee!

Acknowledge Everything You Have Gone Through.

You have gone through so much hardship in your life! Yet you are still living each day, the best you know how. You have spent money on this book to improve your situation. You got up this morning, washed your face and started the day with hope and corn flakes. You helped the kids get ready for school. You threw in a load of wash and swiffered the dog hair under the table.

You are working day and night to have a good life. Yet, you seldom take time to give yourself a pat on the back for all the challenges you have forged through triumphantly.

Close your eyes and take a few moments to really give yourself credit for pressing through those hurtful situations. You made it through. You didn't crumble, you worked through it. Tell yourself that you are proud of you for not giving up, for not breaking down, for not giving in.

No one has lived your life, suffered your pain, felt your individual feelings. Oh, some can relate to what you have gone through, but never exactly what the feelings are. We are all unique and handle things in different ways.

Have a little triumph party for yourself. Buy yourself a gourmet cupcake as a treat and give yourself permission to celebrate all you have been through. Be your own champion and cheerleader! Because of all the situations you have endured, you are self-aware, wise, perceptive, shrewd and utterly amazing.

WASH THAT MOUTH OUT!

We absolutely cannot increase our happiness meter until we are tuned in to how we talk to ourselves about ourselves.

I spent years absorbing and believing the criticism and judgement spoken about me. Deep down I knew I was smart, nice, and had a good sense of humor, but the traits that mattered to those who judged me were beauty, appearance, popularity, and success. All qualities I was lacking.

Hence the words that darted out of my mouth about myself were the same words I heard coming from others.

Criticizing and downgrading myself became normal and no big deal. If someone didn't come down on me for something, you bet your bippy I was first in line for my emotional and verbal beating.

Newsflash: No one is better than anyone else. And no one is less than anyone else (no matter what they tell you). How I felt about myself had to improve and the starting point was my rotten, filthy mouth.

Obviously, this was a foreign concept for me. I was like a toddler giving up her favorite binkie. Even though the way I spoke about myself was not supportive in any way, it was the devil I knew... that creepy, hot, bright-red creature that somehow took control of my mind and in a strange way, I was comfortable with.

Making the conscious choice to pay attention to the words I said to myself was first on the agenda.

Idiot, moron, dingbat, fat, stupid, dumb, jerk, imbecile, ass, loser, failure, no good, worthless, ugly, less than, defective, damaged.

Any time one of those words remotely entered my head, I would stop and attempt to replace it with a gentler description.

Smart, savvy, wise, curious, beautiful, creative, persevering, nice, funny, steadfast, calm, insightful, adventurous, loyal, adaptable, easy going, more than enough, champion, brave.

It helps to keep a journal and jot down how you speak to yourself. Try this for a week. You might be surprised at what pops in your head and runs out of your mouth.

Suggested words to eliminate from your vocabulary:

JUST:

I'm just a housewife.
I just have a GED.
I am just a nobody.
I just make $20K a year.
I'm just an assistant.
I'm just a store employee.
I'm just a stay at home mother.

ONLY:

I'm only down 3 pounds.
I'm only living in this one room apartment.
I'm only making $9 per hour.
I only have one good friend.
I'm only a custodian.
I'm only an average looking person.

IF ONLY:

If only I had a better job.
If only I had my neighbor's house.
If only I had a better childhood.
If only I were a size smaller.
If only I had a more expensive car.
If only I had more education.

BUT:

Thank you, but I have more weight to lose.
Thank you, but I wish I had a better position.
It's okay, but I wish it was curlier.
Thanks, but I found it in the clearance bin.
Thanks, but I'm not that special.
Yeah, but no one will ever love me.

These small words carry a serious amount of power. They negate, berate, and diminish your worth. Be conscious of when you use them and change your phrasing. Be proud of where you are in your life. Your journey is not over. You are working towards getting what you want. Do not downplay yourself or your life. Stand proud.

LOVE YOURSELF…EVEN THE ICKY PARTS

My stomach jiggles. My nose is too long. The operation scar on my stomach is shaped like a question mark. My feet are too wide.

There are things we just don't like about ourselves. The older we get, the longer and droopier the list.

At some point, it's critical to begin an acceptance process of ourselves. We are going to be with ourselves for the rest of our lives and it's about time we make peace with us. All of us. Doesn't mean we have to be perfect, but maybe we should look at our "flaws" differently. Maybe start with finding one thing we can appreciate about that part of ourselves that we despise.

Here's a personal example. Several years back I had an emergency life-saving surgery to remove a growth on my intestines. My sleepy-eyed surgeon was awakened out of a sound sleep to slice me up and remove the angry little bugger. Once healed the scar was, and still is, about 7 inches long and shaped like a question mark. My dreams of becoming a bikini model had been shattered.

I hated that scar!

Then I remembered to attempt to love my icky parts. The truth is, because of this scar I literally have my life. I survived. This scar is a symbolic reminder of how resilient my body is and that I recovered. As 'questionable' as it might seem, I am now grateful for that scar.

Moving on to my wide feet. Even though they are wide, there is this awesome shoe store in the city that exclusively sells wide width shoes. I can get a $150 pair of boots in the off season for $6.96. Thinking about it, I guess I don't care if my feet are three feet wide because I am able to walk around the block and up a flight of stairs. And, as a bonus, my toes are perfectly symmetrical. If my feet were narrower, who knows, my magnificent toe structure might be squashed and distorted. My middle toe could be longer than my fourth toe. My thumb toe could be smaller than my pinky toe. So much to be grateful for!

Try to make peace with the physical attributes you find lacking or repulsive. You might say, "Now hear this bat wing arms, I am grateful to have you! You might sway a little when the wind blows, but you help me carry my groceries, push the baby carriage, tie my shoes and pull up my pants. You may not look like Barbie arms, but you are serving an important purpose."

You might be saying to yourself, "Well, the things I hate about myself are preventing me from getting the man I want."

I distinctly remember a deeply personal conversation with a lovely client of mine. She was searching for love and had a rough stretch of meeting the wrong guys. She felt insecure while dating these men and it did a number on her self-esteem. She was adorable and had a perfect figure. She also was a gracious, intelligent, creative and adventurous young woman. A total package.

During one session she told me she wanted breast implants. She said that she believed her breasts were too small and that is why the men she dated did not want to commit. She convinced herself that her well-proportioned chest was the main reason men left her. She honestly believed that if she had larger breasts, more men would find her attractive and as a result, someone would want to put a ring on it.

My heart went out to her. I saw her beauty. As is. We had a long discussion about self-worth. How important it is to embrace our whole being. To accept what God has given us. To go out into the world putting our best foot forward and looking and feeling our best.

As far as changing appearance, my thought is if you are changing for yourself, more power to you. If your nose reaches the door 8 inches before your lips do and an adjustment would make you feel better about yourself, by all means, go for it! Do it for yourself, because it will make *you* feel better.

But if you are going under the knife for the sole purpose of impressing a man, think twice. It might be time to embrace that imperfection. Slimmer feet will not necessarily snag you a husband.

Love all of you! Every day make note of negative things you say to yourself and think of a positive affirmation. It works and over time, you might realize that you're digging all of yourself!

And by the way, the right person will cherish all of you just the way you are; bat wings, little boobies, wide feet and all!

Mic drop.

BABYSITTERS KNOW BEST

When Becca was 6 years old, I hired a babysitter to watch Becca in our home after school while I was working. Kayla was a high school junior, a poetic young woman who was wise beyond her years. I was told Becca was so well behaved when Kayla watched her, which was every day from 3:30 – 5:30 pm. Kayla was compassionate and attentive. A diamond in the rough.

One day when I came home and relieved Kayla of her duties, she asked to talk to me for a minute.

"Sure, what's up?" I instantly panicked and anticipated the Dear John babysitter speech. Now I've got to go through the whole interview process again, hang up flyers in the school and library, then do background checks and referrals. I don't have time for this.

"Well, I wanted to respectfully talk to you about Becca and the dynamic between you two."

Oh, is that all? Whew, I can handle a chat about my daughter. I'm so glad she's not leaving me!

Kayla started off by telling me what an incredible kid Becca is and how great they get along. She is smart as a whip and a sweet soul. Becca does not cross the line with Kayla and she is respectful and well-mannered.

Wow, this is nice validation for me! This girl is a gem!

Kayla continued. "I sensed for some time how manipulative Becca can be towards you. I have seen you cave many times when Becca whined and would not let up until she got her way. This is after you firmly said

54

"No". Gayle, remember, you are her mother and you should be calling the shots. A 6-year-old should not be getting away with the things she gets away with."

Why didn't she just punch me in the gut?

Then my thought after five seconds of silence: So, this 17-year old kid is telling me how to raise my kid? Telling me I am a rotten, horrible mother? Doesn't she understand I am divorced and doing this all by lonesome? Didn't she notice how nicely I cut Becca's bangs? Did she even acknowledge that Becca eats her fruits and vegetables? Okay, sweetie pie, talk to me when you have your own kids. Just wait. Just wait. I smirked to myself.

Ten seconds later, I took a breath and realized Kayla was right.

I did cave. I neglected to follow through with certain punishments. I had a ferocious bark but when push came to shove, I backed down like a spineless jellyfish. In my defense, I wasn't a pushover in any situation that would put her in danger. If she was about to pour scalding water over her head, you bet your cannoli she'd be scared straight. Or if she ever made fun of another kid, I would not accept any excuse and she would be standing in the corner for at least ten years.

After Kayla left that afternoon, I had a lot to think about. Initially, I tried to convince myself that I was justified for backing down because sometimes the punishment did not fit the crime, and I became soft. But there was a bigger issue here. It took a few days to come to me yet when it did it hit me like a lightning bolt.

After the divorce, my guilt was monumental. I did not want Becca to grow up in a 'broken' home like I did, although her environment might have been worse had we not split. I took my vows seriously and since I knew what it was like to come from a divorced home, I never wanted that for my child.

I felt like I failed her. I guess to make up for my failings, I let her call the shots. Not consciously though. I did not make an announcement "HERE YE HERE YE now that I'm divorced I will allow my daughter to do whatever she wants whenever she wants until her babysitter will have to knock some sense into me!"

I guess I overcompensated so she wouldn't be sad or upset in any way. I must have believed that any time she pitched a fit it was because she was hurting from the divorce, not because she was a typical child who didn't get what she wanted. When she flung the Candyland gingerbread pieces all over the living room because she didn't win, was it anger stemming from our divorce three years ago or a tantrum due to her first board game loss as an only child.

Bottom line, I did not want her to be upset, and if I'm truly honest, I did not want her to be upset with me. So, I gave her the power. I empowered this adorable little wide-eyed squirt to run the world and our little household.

Changes had to be made. I spent a considerable amount of time thinking about the behaviors that needed reigning in and how to deal with them. I made a chart with adorable stickers and wrote the top three situations that drove me crazy: Bedtime fits, having the last word, and not putting away her toys. I talked straight up and calmly told her that there would be consequences for her actions. I told her what the punishment would be if she talked back and told her there would be a warning before she would have the consequence.

It took a little time for both of us to get used to this new way of living, but it worked like a charm. That homemade chart was taped to the refrigerator and Becca knew exactly which of her favorite toys would be taken away if she didn't clean up her room when asked. The beauty was I did not have to make up a punishment on the fly. Everything was in black and white and easy for me to follow. And I did not feel guilty. It felt right.

Thanks Kayla, you were instrumental in helping Becca become the phenomenal woman she is today.

SILENCE IS GOLDEN

Sitting still for more than five minutes. No TV. No radio. No vodka. No sound. No way. I'd rather have tarantulas crawl on my face.

Being still. Not one of my strengths. After the split, I was on the move. Faster than a speeding bullet. I went out every single night when Becca was with her dad. I was fortunate to have amazing friends from work that I hung out with. They were a tremendous support system for me. Living in overdrive, doing nine things at once, making plans for every minute of every day. It was virtually impossible for me to sit still and just be. Oh, I could watch television for hours, but to sit on the sofa, close my eyes and be silent? No way. Bring on the critters.

After several months of this unhealthy, yet very lively, road-runner lifestyle, it dawned on me that I should start spending time on my own. If not, it was inevitable that I'd be asked to pay rent at my favorite watering hole. I was never going to leave me, so I might as well take baby steps, spend some time alone and start appreciating the woman who slept with me, wore my clothes, loved chocolate chip cookies and forged through so many hardships.

Why was being still and quiet so important? I have realized that there is a faint voice way down deep in my belly that guides my path. The whisper that keeps my standards high and integrity in check. The certain knowing of whether to wait or take a step forward. The deep faith that God is with me and all will be okay, no matter what. That pause when I am at a critical juncture and need to make a discerning decision. The stillness grounds me, centers me.

I cannot count how many times I have struggled for answers in my frenzied state, but when I quieted down and took a breath, an answer finally came. Maybe not in that exact moment, but it calmed me enough to be patient and wait. When the answer did come I was confident it is the right answer. What has failed me time and time again is when I make an impulsive decision out of panic or fear, not out of peace.

Silent time helps me connect with God and trust His will.

It took me literally months of attempts to finally get comfortable sitting in silence for a reasonable amount of time. At first, I lasted less than a minute – fidgety and restless, wet-noodling off the couch like a 2-year old, contorting a paperclip into an elephant. Focus Gayle! I tried again and again. Hey, I sat still for 18 seconds! Then 42 seconds. It's a process.

I have evolved and now I crave quiet time.

Generally, I like to spend this sacred time in a squishy chair in my sunflower-filled office, yet sometimes I'll venture out to a deer forest within a nearby zoo. I bring lots of quarters, fill a baggie with corn from the machines, sit on a rock and wait for the deer to come over to me and nudge my arm to be fed. It is here where I become one with nature. These gorgeous creatures walk right up to me with their beautiful doe eyes and I melt as they slobber all over my hand to gobble up every kernel.

My second favorite destination is a small chapel high on a hill. The grounds are majestic with meticulously kept gardens. There are life-sized stations of the cross and at the top of the hill there is a statue of Our Blessed Mother with Bernadette kneeling and gazing up at her. These pure white figures are tucked in a small cove surrounded by huge rocks. The sun shines on them as if they are glowing. It is beyond serene. There is an innocence and honesty about this scene that brings me back to basics. It feels like heaven.

It is here where I have heartfelt and brutally honest talks with God, inspiring thoughts, answers that seem to just appear out of nowhere and a deep understanding of exactly what I'm supposed to do. I am safe. In this calm state, I can release fears, pray, reveal my heart, and listen to that gentle voice that guides me. Most times an overwhelming sense of peace calms me and assures me all will be okay.

Answers come in quiet. Answers don't penetrate through chaos.

I now cherish the stillness and seek out serene places when I am sad, challenged, disappointed, hopeless, discouraged, or depressed. The silence helps me break through these negative feelings and allows me to feel a sense of understanding that there is a higher force at work in my life. I trust that feeling. Sitting in stillness is a blessing and a gift.

I will pray and ask God for help.

God, please shut all the doors that are not right for me and open all the doors that are Your will.

God, please help me to discern the difference between Your will and my will.

God, please help me hear You.

God, please help me love myself.

God, please help me find my true essence.

God, please help me not be so frustrated by this situation.

God, please help me learn to eat healthier.

God, please help me to accept where I'm at even though I'm not where I want to be.

God, please help me make the right decision in this painful situation.

God, please help me learn the lesson during this grim time.

God, please help me serve and bless others.

God, please put people in my path who You want me to help, sot that I may do Your work.

God, please help me forgive those who hurt me.

God, please help me want to do what is right.

God, please give me the strength to be gracious and patient.

God, please protect those who are going through a traumatic experience.

Give them peace and strength to handle it.

God, thank You for all the blessings in my life.

Thank You for giving me the courage to live life with You by my side.

PAIN IS PAIN

* Splitting up is painful.

* Watching your child suffer is painful.

* Being passed over for that promotion is painful.

* Saying goodbye to a friend moving out of town is painful.

* Loneliness is painful.

* Watching the one you love date another is painful.

* Being the object of gossip is painful.

Pain is pain, regardless of how it shows up. We often put down our pain if we feel someone else's pain is worse than ours. It is heartfelt to show compassion to a loved one who is hurting, but don't diminish your own pain. Whatever degree you think your pain is – from a small hurt or a big ordeal - it is real. And you are hurting because of it. Acknowledge your pain.

On the other hand, you might be going through something very painful to you, yet a loved one is in pain over something you feel is not as significant. Even though her situation is not as tragic or intense as what you are dealing with, always remember that her pain is real also. Be sensitive to the lesser pains as well.

Compassion is needed everywhere. A supportive word, a gentle hug or an invitation for a venting session with a cup of tea or box of wine can lessen the sting of any type of pain. Pain is pain no matter what its cause.

RECEIVE, YES, YOU!

We work our fingers to the bone, struggle to pay all the bills but manage to do it, bring home the bacon and fry it up in a pan, then the moment someone takes notice and praises us, we minimize our accomplishments and downplay everything we've ever done.

"Oh, honey, it was no big deal."

"That's what a mother is supposed to do!"

"He will never go out with me. I'm not good enough."

"I didn't make the entire Thanksgiving meal from scratch. I feel so worthless!"

Stop it! Stop downplaying your worth! Stop apologizing for not doing more! Stop it! Stop it! Stop it!

Woman are nurturers by nature. We see a baby and immediately want to snug him and take care of him. We don't fall asleep until everyone is safe and sound under their blankies. We care for a sick family member even though we just had a root canal and are hobbling around on a broken leg. Because many of us were raised to believe that life was about sacrificing for others, we never learned how to embrace our own moments to shine.

I plead with you to become aware of how you do not receive. Please be aware of how you respond to others that want to give to you, whether it be a compliment or assistance.

This could be your response when someone wants to help you. (It's no coincidence that they all begin with OH NO!):

- Oh no, that's okay. I can take care of it myself.
- Oh no, I don't want to put you out.
- Oh no, you have your own family, don't worry about me.
- Oh no, I can handle it.
- Oh no, that's too much money.
- Oh no, you don't have to do that! I'm fine.
- Oh no, you're too busy.
- Oh no, I don't really need it.

The person offering you help wishes you would accept their loving gesture. They want to make things easier for you and show you they care. They want to take the heavy burden from you.

Yet, you will not receive.

Receiving is an act of self-love. It might be hard to do, but you deserve the compassion that others want to give you.

Several years ago, my dad and step mother had back to back cancers. Both forged through chemo and radiation. Both are strong. I live an hour away and wanted to help during this troublesome time. I mentioned that I wanted to buy them frozen prepared meals so they could just pop them in the oven whenever they wanted. As we all know, chemo and radiation come with the dreadful side effects of nausea, vomiting and exhaustion and I thought having these easy to prepare meals would make life a bit easier for them.

They both said no. (See above for the OH NO responses.)

I loved them and wanted to help. I could not take away their pain or make them feel any better. This was something I could do to make their lives a bit easier. So, against their wishes, I ordered two weeks-worth of frozen meals. They were delivered directly to their home so they could not turn them away.

A few days later I met Daddy for dinner. He said, "You know honey, I really enjoyed that turkey pot pie and meatloaf dinner you sent us. It was delicious! We appreciate it."

I was thrilled! The only thing that would have made me happier is if they had **received** and accepted my desire to help right away and I didn't have to jump through hoops to get them to agree!

Think of a time when you wanted to do something thoughtful for someone you love and they wouldn't accept it. You wanted to show you cared but they didn't want to put you out. Totally frustrating, right? Yeah, right.

Accept giving gestures. You are cherished. Receive the compassion and tenderness you deserve.

Let others show how much they love you, just as you would do for someone you love!

PULL IT OUT!

Oh, get your mind out of the gutter, I'm talking about glassware.

We've all heard the idea of using our fancy wedding gifts in our everyday life, but have you ever eaten Spaghetti O's out of a Baccarat Crystal bowl? Or worn that Tiffany's diamond necklace to the movies? Or wiped mustard off your face with a designer linen napkin...on a Tuesday?

What a great concept! Until now, I never had the courage to implement it. I didn't want to break a $298 dish or get gravy stains on a hand stenciled tablecloth, so I left these items tucked away under the cobwebs for that special occasion. After creating a whole new life, I decided to dig out that Waterford dish and put some M&Ms in it.

And just like that, something extraordinary happened. I put a few M&Ms in my mouth and they tasted better! The assortment of colors in the crystal dish as the sun shone through produced vibrant rainbow colors on my floor. They looked more appealing in the translucent dish rather than in a warped plastic bowl. Maybe there was something to this idea after all.

What other forgotten treasures can I dig out of the basement and start using? The fear of dropping a valuable piece of...whatever... vanished when I began to unearth antique items under hairballs and dead flies. Who said anything beautiful must be kept on the top shelf in the back of a closet behind the luggage until celebrating a special occasion? I began wearing some of my fancy only-wear-on-my-anniversary undie and bra sets instead of the combos with holes, missing clasps, stains and worn elastic. I put on a normal outfit over my lacey undergarments, and instantly I felt tres chic and sexy!

My friend dresses up in her blingiest gown, stilettos, makeup and dazzling earrings during the Oscars. She's not sitting next to Denzel in LA, she's on her living room sofa watching on TV. My other friend woke up at 5:30 am to watch the royal wedding in her pajamas and a fascinator. Way to embrace these events!

It's important to put beauty around you because you are worth it. You probably have everything at your disposal in the back of the closet.

- Who says Christmas lights should only be used at Christmas? Wrap a string of white lights around an indoor plant or hang a few strands around the edge of the ceiling in your sunroom.
- Wear the heirloom pin that you inherited from Gram. It will be a nice remembrance of her and would look lovely on your black coat.
- Put your favorite Lladro in plain view.
- Cut flowers from your garden and place them all over the house.
- Drink a glass of milk out of the His and Hers Champagne glasses you toasted with at your wedding.
- Put on berry blossom lipstick before filling up your gas tank.
- Loofah and lotion your body with special products even if you're hanging out at home.
- Prepare a sacred spot in your home that is yours only. A comfy chair, a scented candle, a bubbling water fountain; paint the area in a favorite color, add some nice light with vibrant colors, incense, anything that you find relaxing and peaceful. Hell, put a copy of this book there to inspire you and motivate you to be your best self!

It may sound goofy to wear your fancy schmancy earrings to the grocery store, but I believe in the principal of it. Why not take it up a notch when you go to the store? There is nothing wrong with doing things that make you feel good and putting things around you that are pleasing to the eye.

You are not doing these things for anyone else. You are doing them for yourself. And wait until you elevate the taste of those Cheese Doos served in your Lenox dish! Nummy!

MOOLAH

Or I should say lack of. Let's face it, when you go from two incomes to one, this causes a financial upheaval. Where there used to be two incomes to pay the mortgage, electric bill, phone bill, and grocery bills, there is now one. I needed to come up with some imaginative ways to embrace life on a low budget.

Here are a few low-cost ideas to maintain some type of normalcy when you're financially strapped.

- Picnic in the park. Grab a blanket, snacks, drinks, music and lettuce to feed the ducks. Remove your shoes and walk barefoot on the grass, lie down on the blanket, look up at the sky, breathe in and out appreciating your surroundings. And of course, people watch. You will always witness intriguing sights at the park.
- Movie night. After the kids are in their jammies, pick out a movie that all will enjoy! Shut all the lights, make popcorn or cookies, find a snugly spot on the sofa with a fleece throw and fluffy pillow. No cell phones, no iPad, no computer, no distractions.
- Check your local newspapers for free family days. Museums, parks, tasting events are available during all seasons for minimal or no charge.
- Carve out special time for tickling and hugging your kids. Precious moments with my daughter kissing her all over the face and pinching her little belly. That laughter! That toothy grin! No money can buy that!
- Listen to music. Download a few of your favorites and play them whenever you are gloomy. This small activity will give you joy, help you grieve, force out tears, entice you to dance. I

had my hard rock songs to jam to in the car, easy listening while in the tub, opera when introspective, and pop songs in the kitchen while making dinner.

- Go to a drive-in movie. Gather your kids and lawn chairs and watch a triple treat. Fold back the seats in the van, bring fleece blankets, snacks, drinks and pillows from home. A sure win for a fabulous night out!
- Visit a hot air balloon festival or an air show. They are up in the sky so find a place you can see them for free.
- Build a campfire. Get some graham crackers, marshmallows and chocolate bars and tell ghost stories. Spooky!
- Walk or hike in the woods. Nothing like breathing in fresh air and getting your heart rate up. Sit on a rock near a stream and listen to the bubbling. Invigorating!
- Search for spare change. Look under the sofa cushions, in the dryer, in winter coat pockets, in last season's jeans, under the car seat, there's sure to be some cash somewhere. I remember doing this and finding $17.67, enough for pizza night!
- Read. Curl up with a cup of tea and Biscotti. Get lost in a fantasy or discover ways to save the planet. Immerse yourself.
- Ask a friend to visit. We might get lonely and all it takes is a text and some chips and salsa for a pleasant evening! Reach out to someone who also might want some company.
- Take a nap! Rest, regroup, regenerate, refuel, replenish.
- Watch a funny video. Watching an old Robin Williams comedy special is an ideal way to shift your mood.
- Dabble in the Arts. Take up knitting, cross stitch or latch hooking. Sign up for a night life class to learn pottery, stained glass, make Italian meatballs, belly dance, paint by numbers. Creative possibilities are endless.
- Beach it!
- Go to a library book swap event! Bring one, receive one!
- Visit a local museum. Even if it is a place you normally would not frequent, you might develop an appreciation for the artists'

work and talent.

- Join a club. Women's, men's, charitable, service, meet-ups, seniors, Lion's. Check your local information for clubs in your area. What a clever way to meet new acquaintances and feel a sense of community!
- Go fishing. Borrow a rod, dig up some worms, cast away and wait for a nibble.
- Go to a children's park and swing as high as you can and then teeter on the totter. Become childlike for an afternoon.
- Smell the flowers. If you are walking around in May, sniff a nearby lilac bush. In August, inhale the fragrant smell of roses (make sure it's bee-free). Each month has a new season of fresh flowers. Seek them out and take a whiff!
- Lie on a hammock. Place it between two trees, add a pillow and smell the fresh grass and gaze up at the blue sky.
- Make homemade pizza or cupcakes. Let the kids pile on the pepperoni and sprinkles!
- Dance naked. Sometimes feeling uninhibited is wildly exciting and invigorating! If you are uncomfortable, shut the lights, close the blinds and stay away from the mirror.
- Blow bubbles. Best low-cost activity ever!
- Putz around a consignment shop or yard sale. Even if you only have a few bucks to spare, you might find amazing treasures. I went to a consignment shop and bought a crystal bowl for $22. I googled the cut glass and it was worth $540! My friend bought a real Louboutin pocketbook for $5! Or sign up to consign your goodies that are collecting dust. Shrewd way to earn a few extra buckaroos.
- Go to a free concert on the common. Swing bands, barbershop quartets, high school choirs, square dancing.
- Ride your bicycle. Take a spin to the post office or around the neighborhood. One of my fondest childhood memories was going on family bike rides.
- Throw a frisbee, play pool, wiffleball or ping pong, put up a net

and play soccer or volleyball in the backyard.

- Cuddle with your pet. Pet them, massage them, rub their belly, kiss their forehead, play with their jelly bean toes.
- Give the kids some chalk and let them have a ball on the driveway.
- Have poker night with friends. Ask everyone to bring an appetizer and their preferred spirits.
- Go to a movie theatre that shows older movies. The price of the show is usually under $5.00.
- Do some household things you've been putting off; clean your cruddy oven; bag up clothes that you will never squeeze into again; stain that antique table that's been taking up space in the basement; touch up the scuff marks around the house.
- Take pictures of butterflies, the sky, an earthworm, a little league game, a sunset, an old log, your favorite dish. Anything that ignites the artist in you!
- Adopt an animal (It will cost initially, but in the long run, it will be so worth it!)
- Take a joy ride. Explore streets you've never been on. If you see water on the GPS, put your directional on and check out the stately homes on the lake.
- Walk around a farm and feed the animals. We have a little farm/ice cream place about ½ hour from my house. It sits atop a mountain. The ice cream is homemade and oh so creamy. Wear stretchy pants!
- Stop by a lake with a head of lettuce and feed the swans.
- Bored on a Sunday afternoon? Visit open houses in surrounding towns and soak up creative ideas. It can give you motivation to paint a room or rearrange furniture
- Color in a coloring book. It's relaxing. It's relaxing. It's relaxing.
- Pitch a tent outside and have an outdoor sleep. It might be labor intensive, but the kids will relish in the adventure!
- Stay up late and look at the stars. It's peaceful and you

appreciate the enormity of the universe. Look for the dippers! (I originally typed diapers here. Lol!)

- Buy something unique every time you to the grocery store. It's adventurous to try new foods. Hey Mikey, he likes it!
- Go kayaking. Feel blissful on a quiet lake. Bring gloves and a cushion for your bum.
- Visit a town fair. Putz around looking at local vendor goodies. Taste test. Meet some new neighbors. Chomp on a fresh cuke.
- Plant a garden.
- Have a snow ball fight or grab a cafeteria tray and slide down a snowy hill.
- Sit outside on your porch during a thunderstorm. Shut your eyes and listen to the rain plop on the roof.
- Relax in a place of worship. Quiet your mind. Pray. Light a candle. Forgive. Leave it in God's hands.
- Give yourself a manicure and pedicure.
- Sell brownies and lemonade with your kids on a scorching summer afternoon. Find a well-traveled road and let your kids buy themselves a treat with all the cash they made!
- Make a special recipe. A hand me down, grandma's apple pie, aunt yoyo's crab dip, Uncle Joe's cow tongue.
- Put up a bird feeder and watch them flutter around and gobble up all the seeds.
- Take a hard look at everything you spend money on and take action to lower your bills. Call the cable company, phone and internet providers and try to get a lower rate. Rip up credit cards, except for an emergency one. Transfer existing balances to 0 percent credit cards. Bring your lunch to work. Limit Starbucks runs. Don't exceed your allowed spending money for the week. Make a list when you shop so you don't pick up unnecessary items. Don't grocery shop when you are hungry (big mistake...*big!*). Barter with friends: You cut and color my hair and I'll watch your kids for a night.

I have thought about money quite a bit and most of us think that the more expensive something is, the better it is. But that is not always the case.

Recently, I was sitting on a dock on a river. A huge yacht cruised by. It was three stories high and had at least ten passengers sunbathing outside. This was a stellar and exquisite piece of equipment.

A few minutes later, a beat-up old rowboat popped out of a cove. The dilapidated dinghy was in dire need of a paint job and an elderly couple sat face to face inside. They had a cooler in between them and perched on the front of the boat was the American flag. They rowed by me and shouted a big Hello! As the yacht slowly traveled along the middle of the river, the rowboat turned left into a narrow stream. In the stream were breathtaking sights of rare white birds.

The yacht members might have splurged on caviar and champagne and floated in luxury, and the rowboat passengers might have had peanut butter and jelly sandwiches and Miller Lite, but it was the tired, beat up rowboat that squeezed in that stream so they could experience the gorgeous flight of those rare white birds.

More expensive doesn't necessarily mean better or more memorable. Make the best of what you have. It's enough...and sometimes smaller is even better.

Stepping Out In Love

Part 2

THE TURBULENT SINGLE ROAD

OH, THE THINGS I CAN DO!

Being single comes with its own type of freedom. Rather than focusing on what I lost, I choose to make a list of the things I can do! As a single person, I can:

- eat gummy bears for dinner
- take 5 hours getting ready to go out
- dip my toe in the lady pond if I am so inclined
- buy more pocketbooks and shoes…just because
- use the potty without shutting the door (but not in public, and not when I have eaten asparagus because my cats will come charging in the bathroom)
- watch a movie without blood, guts, robots, or boobies
- go to bed at 3 am and wake up at 1 pm
- never ever worry about falling in the toilet at 2 am because someone left the seat up
- fill every inch of every closet in the house
- paint the living room a bold shade of twinkly princess pink
- get a tattoo of Ryan Reynolds on my back
- donate the hair on my legs to Locks for Love
- adopt a rescue dog with 1 eye, 3 legs and a chronic dingleberry
- get in my jammies at 4 pm and let my clothes drop to the floor… and leave them there!
- sleep sideways in my king-sized bed using all four pillows
- come home to a house exactly how I left it that morning
- round up to the nearest dollar in my checkbook
- go for a week without turning on the telly
- Fill the house with incense, drum music and big floor pillows
- eat breakfast in the tub

So many things to be, do, and try!

THERE'S MORE TO LIFE THAN BRUSHING

Somewhere along the way, we have settled into a routine of getting up, brushing our teeth, going to work, making supper, watching TV, brushing our teeth, going to bed and then doing it all over again the next day. And the next. Weekends might be reserved for washing the floors, doing laundry, ironing the curtains, vacuuming the furniture and prepping food for the upcoming week. You might catch up on sleep or watch that movie for the 10th time. There is nothing wrong with doing these things, in fact, most are necessary, but you have this nagging voice telling you that there has got to be more to life than this.

You used to feel a fire ignite in your belly when you thought of all the possibilities out there.

Now your thought process might go something like this:

"I'm too old to dream that dream. I don't have enough money to get that degree. I don't have time to spend pampering myself, I have so many other things to take care of. There are not enough hours in the day. I'd love to volunteer but the little I can do won't make any impact. I've always wanted to try out for a local theatre production, but I've never acted in front of an audience. I would love to enroll in an advanced painting class but I'm exhausted when I get home. I am fascinated with crystals but my friends will think it's strange if I took a class. I'd be thrilled to publish my poetry but who would read it?! But... But... But..."

Because of this negative self-talk, we settle and stuff our true desires in the back of our minds and the bottom of our souls. Like those ornate candle holders that are forgotten in the basement underneath a bunch of dryer lint pieces. Next day we get up, brush our teeth, go to work, make supper, watch TV, go to bed, then do it all over again.

So many activities we'd be willing to try yet we are held back. Or rather, we hold *ourselves* back.

If you think of a child, his natural tendency is to be curious about everything! If you sit with a toddler for an hour, you will watch him climb on furniture, put toys in his mouth, knock down blocks, watch the bright colors on TV, climb in the Tupperware cupboard, try to open the baggie with his Cheerios in it, dance to the Piggly Wiggly song, and stack plastic donuts. You'll probably have to clean the soggy wet spots off the couch, your jeans, and the wallpaper because he likes to touch everything. My point is that little ones are so excited about new experiences and their curiosity leads them to stumble upon all sorts of cool stuff! Every day they learn something new.

For some strange reason, as we become grown-ups, our passion, desire, and curiosity fades. We get into a rut, a lifestyle which sometimes keeps us stuck in the same place for years.

Just a thought. Now that you are on your own, even if you have kids, take some steps and become curious yourself.

Nothing great ever happens while brushing your teeth. Greatness happens when you go after what you want. At the end of your life, you don't want to regret those chances you didn't take.

Get in touch with that adventurous child inside of you and let your curiosity soar! Life is more exciting when you decide to get up and dance to the Piggly Wiggly!

ROMANTIC LOVE VS. PUPPY LOVE

What's the difference?

We all have the capability to love and be loved. Love comes in so many thrilling, intriguing, luxurious, delicious shapes and sizes.

- Listening to a toddler's laughter
- Watching a highly rated rotten tomatoes Netflix series
- Napping on an overcast, dreary afternoon, or any day of the week
- Sipping cocoa with butterscotch schnapps
- Watching Becca's face light up when I tell her how proud I am of her, for no reason at all
- Going to a Broadway play and dining at a fabulous restaurant
- Witnessing the growth of my coaching clients
- Laughing until my face hurts, I snort, or pee a little; whichever comes first
- Gazing at the elegance of a swan
- Unhooking my bra after a long day at work
- Soaking up an elderly person's wisdom and stories

All these things make me feel warm and gooey inside. They put me in touch with a deeper, more meaningful joy. They simply make life better.

So, why is it that the type of love I valued most of all was the love of a man? It was like all other love diminished in its ability to fill me up. I put all my focus in obtaining the adoration of a man. I thought that a male's attention and affection was better than any other type of love.

Whether I had a man's love or not should not make a puppy less appealing to me, but in theory, it did.

This was quite a lesson for me. Like a bonk on the head lesson. Who would ever imagine the insane concept that love is love, no matter what vessel it shows up in. I confess I did not fully recognize the value of the love that was standing right in front of me.

I thought a man's love was somehow higher on the love chain than other types of love. Family love, friend love, child love, pet love, nature love, chocolate love, bubble bath love, higher power love, running love, Italian meatball love, tennis love, gardening love, poetry love, dancing love, horse-riding love and flea market love. I was too focused on finding the love of a desirable partner and not fully connected to love that was all around me. I downplayed those moments when they occurred and thought, "Yeah that was a sweet gesture, but it wasn't from a man, and that's what I really want. That is the love that really matters." Oh, poor me. Poor blind me. It was time to open my eyes.

That thought process had me paralyzed, big time. Once I accepted that love is love no matter what shape or form it shows itself in, I broke free and became more appreciative of all the blessings surrounding me.

Love is love. It is not one specific person, animal, task, event or action. It is what fills you up, ignites your passion, tickles your fancy, makes the hair on your neck stand up, awakens butterflies in your belly, gives you confidence, heightens your senses, relaxes you, and makes you want to share your big smile with the world.

Receive the gift of love and don't worry about what form it comes in. Love is all around, in all shapes and sizes. It abounds!

ROUTINES

After our split, I was super mindful about maintaining as much normalcy in our lives, especially for my 4-year old daughter, Becca. Life as she knew it would never be the same and I wanted to make this difficult transition as painless as possible. So if there was something, anything, I could do to make things remain the same, I would do that.

I had reluctantly accepted the notion that once we went our separate ways we would sell our house and I would move to a small apartment or condominium. I absolutely dreaded the thought of moving, but felt I had no choice because I could not afford to buy my ex out. The idea of moving out and uprooting Becca from her home was tearing me apart.

After a few months of racking my brain trying to come up with some type of plan to stay in the house, a solution came out of nowhere at 3 am. I woke from a sound sleep, sat straight up in bed and figured how to get the money that would allow us to remain in the house. I remembered my 401k account had decent money in it. I could withdraw the funds, pay my ex his share of the appraised value of the house and refinance to a lower interest rate. These changes would be enough to pay the mortgage and bills.

Anyone and everyone advised me not to withdraw the money from my 401k. There would be penalties on top of penalties, tax implications, and the obvious, my retirement savings would be kaput. But I stood my ground. My stubbornness resulted in several heated conversations with people I respected and relied on for sound advice. Keeping Becca in her home meant everything to me in that moment. I was 34 years old. I had plenty of time to re-build my retirement savings. Looking back, it was the best decision I ever made. No regrets.

I'm not sure if life would have been drastically different had I moved to an apartment down the street, but I was relieved to be able to give Becca the stability of staying in her home.

In my mind, providing a consistent lifestyle was critical. Not so stringent that we had to do the same thing each day, but to participate in activities she could count on that were familiar to her. We would go to a local park at least once or twice a week, soccer practice on weeknights, games on the weekends. On Thursdays, we would to go Papa Gino's with my friend Cindy and her kids and they would color and do arts and crafts. Since we were creating a new life, I wanted her to feel comfortable with the activities we were doing and also feel safe with our altered lifestyle.

There were several neighborhood kids that were Becca's age. She played with our neighbor Wyatt quite a bit. He was a year or so younger and they got along great. They would play dress up and board games for hours! Such happy times. They would ride their electronic cars around the cul-de-sac. She in her pink princess car, he in his Batman car. I would set up scavenger hunts for her friends and give out little prizes. We'd bake cookies, watch every Disney movie made, have sleepovers.

I did all I could to keep her life stable and consistent. I have every hope that she will look back on this time with joy.

GIVE BACK

Initially I thought volunteering was a sacrifice I was making for others and they would be the only ones benefiting from my giving. Oh boy, was I wrong about that! My service to others has given me so much more than I could have ever dreamed!

Years ago, I attended a Bible study class and the pastor mentioned he would buy Dunkin Donuts, McDonalds or Subway gift cards in $2 or $5 denominations and would hand them out to those in need. Personally, I felt bad for the homeless and wanted to help but I had this nagging feeling that my money would be spent on alcohol, cigarettes or drugs. So, I refrained from giving. This gift card idea was fabulous!

Recently, I posted on Facebook that I randomly gave a $5 Dunkin Donut gift card to a woman working at a convenient store. The response to the post was overwhelming! I think the reason it was so impactful was because it was a reminder that small gestures we do for others can really make a difference in someone's life.

I stopped in the convenient store to buy a gallon of milk. The woman, in her early 60's I'd guess, was mopping the floor near the entrance. I hesitated before crossing the clean, wet floor and she said, "Oh honey, come on in, don't worry about the floor! I mop 4 or 5 times a shift!" She smiled a big gummy smile, she only had one tooth, lower left. It was warm out and she was sweating through her shirt. She looked worn out and exhausted. I went out to the car and grabbed a gift card from my stash (I keep them in my car so when I'm out and about I'll have them handy). I handed her $5 and told her to get herself a little treat. Her reaction was, "Oh no! You don't have to do that!" I put it in her hand, stared in her tired eyes and said it's just a little blessing for you. She smiled, hugged me and when I looked at her after her hug, her nose started to turn red and her eyes welled up with tears. I had a hunch she had not experienced much random kindness in her life.

Stepping Out In Love

Since I couldn't afford to build a school in Haiti, I didn't think I could do anything that would matter much. I know differently now. The seemingly insignificant things we do for others can inspire, heal, encourage and give hope. That is a fact.

Clean out the mudroom closet, bedroom closet, basement and donate your old clothes; donate your books, gently used bras, shoes, winter hats, gloves and coats; pay for someone's coffee or toll or a coworkers lunch; give a hefty tip; let the person go before you in line, bake cupcakes for a fundraiser, knit a sweater for a senior center craft fair, help an elderly person with her groceries, bring in a coffee cake for your staff, bring coloring books and crayons to the children's floor of a hospital, give away that lawn furniture you haven't used in a decade, give your pots and pans to a recent college graduate, send a baby blanket to an old babysitter who just became a mom, make a commitment to randomly give out gift cards. So many options!

I read about a person who paid the bill for a family with a disabled child. She posted that she had no idea what it was like having a child with special needs, but she was sure that they had medical expenses and challenges unlike other families. Her treat might make their day.

Not long after reading this, I was in a restaurant seated near a family of 5 with a young teen in a wheelchair. I immediately thought this was a perfect opportunity to bless this family and pick up the tab. My initial reaction was to pay for them, then my stinky brain got in the way and tried to talk me out of it. "Wow that's going to be an expensive bill." "You don't even know them Gayle, why on earth would you spend your hard-earned money on strangers? They won't ever do anything for you!" "What a ridiculous idea, do you know how many pocketbooks you can buy with that money you are giving away?"

Our thoughts will do this to us, trying to change our minds about giving and keeping us comfy in our bubble. But I remembered that post and the day I read it I promised myself I would take action and give when I could. And I certainly could. Honestly, it stung a bit to hand my credit card over to the waitress asking her to put their lunch on my card, but as soon as I paid, I felt giddy inside. I couldn't remove the big grin on my face. I remained anonymous and left the restaurant. In the big picture, it was just a lunch, but I think they might have appreciated getting a freebie that day. And it felt so satisfying to be able to help lighten their load for that one meal. For that one moment.

Whatever you choose, just freaking do it. Those clothes and household items that are sitting in your home will not rise and float out of your front door and land in a nearby shelter. You are not helping anyone if you don't physically bag them up, put them in your trunk, drive to the location and give them away.

A million well-intended thoughts don't mean a thing if they are never put into action.

Looking at my life, I'm sure I take the simplest things for granted. I've never personally experienced what it's like to struggle, really struggle, financially. I am so lucky to have a well-paying job, clothes, food, a home, ability to buy gifts and so much more. The blessings I take for granted may be an enormous gift to someone else.

I do, however, need to consciously remind myself to think outside my 'bubble' and grasp the fact that everyone is not as lucky as me. I am surrounded by friends and family that basically have a similar lifestyle. When *like* people are all around me, it's easy to lose sight of the fact that there are so many in need. I can easily get complacent in my thoughts that everyone is just as fortunate.

When I serve food for the homeless, I am leaving my 'bubble' and witnessing need first hand. What is completely amazing to me is the warmth and appreciation I receive from those served. A simple task such as scooping out stew into a plastic bowl garners so much thankfulness from the recipient. Women stand in the freezing cold with their young children waiting patiently after the mid-day prayer to be given a hot meal. When the mother reaches me in line, her eyes say it all. I'm sure years ago she never imagined she and her children would be living this life. She could have been raised in a family just like mine. Makes me really think. I bring along bottles of bubbles for the children and it's as if I had given them a puppy.

These experiences have changed me and increase my desire to help and offer support. Intentionally signing up to donate a few boxes of stuffing and a turkey at Thanksgiving will allow a family to have a special feast. If you had not been so generous, they would not experience what most of us take for granted. This type of giving is powerful.

Each year my church donates to the Samaritan's Purse, Operation Christmas Child. They request shoe boxes filled with crayons, puzzles, glue sticks, pens, toothbrushes, shampoo, stickers etc. for children living in poverty. These are children who will receive one gift for Christmas. This shoebox. That's it.

Fill up a bag with toothbrush, toothpaste, deodorant, t-shirt, life savers, dry shampoo, cards, small notebook and pen, socks, hat, aspirin, and other goodies. Keep it in your car and when you see a homeless person, bless away!

One of my friend's mom died and on her mother's birthday she posted a Random Act of Kindness Day event on Facebook and asked everyone to do something for someone else in honor of her mom.

Might just have to steal that idea! Imagine if you did too!

CHOOSE DIFFERENTLY

Let's say you are in high school English class. Your assignment is to read a novel for homework and you will be tested on it. You decide not to read it and are disappointed with the test results.

What is the solution to this problem? Cheat off your neighbor and get suspended? The obvious answer is to make a different decision about completing your work. If you continue to choose not to do the work, the outcome will be bleak. If you decide to do the work, your outcome will be successful.

In terms of our dating selection process, we cannot expect to pick the same type of unavailable, untrustworthy, unreliable, selfish, deceitful, abusive partner and expect to live in bliss. Yet so many of us do this exact thing. We break up and then soon after we choose the same type of person thinking, "This time it will be different!"

Sorry honey buns, it will not be different.

We are either miserable while sticking it out, blame our partners for being the way they are, or wallow in pain at the thought of another imminent breakup.

I encourage you to choose differently.

At this moment you might be thinking, "I like a certain type." "I'm drawn to the man who has a six pack and loads of cash, but he barely gives me the time of day." "I am drawn to a woman who likes to party, although she parties 4-5 times a week!" "I'm attracted to charismatic, smooth talking, standoffish men who love other women." "He will eventually leave his wife." "I am only sexually attracted to women who are size 2 and under, yet sometimes they are high maintenance."

Yes, we all have our "type" and people we are naturally drawn to. Yet if those people have not made you happy in the past, consider widening your scope. For example, if you only date men that are 6' and taller, maybe you can be open to dating someone a bit shorter. You may be missing out on a whole slew of men who will adore you, treat you right and will be your ideal mate. If you only date women who are red-headed and large chested, maybe you can be open to dating a brunette who is athletic, smart and endearing.

You might be thinking, "I was abused as a child and all I am comfortable with is being with someone who puts me down, ignores me, and criticizes me. In a strange way, this type of person is who I am most familiar with. I might not like it, but I don't know any other way. I usually pick men who gawk at other women and have a volatile temper." Let me tell you that you can choose another way. Being with a quality person who values you might not be familiar territory for you, but it is what you deserve. No matter how others treated you in the past. You deserve to be treated with honor, respect and compassion. Nothing less. If you want to be treated right, you must treat yourself right first. Choose differently sweetheart, you are worth it.

We can go to the other extreme also. So often after a painful breakup and we begin to date again, we brutally pick apart the perfectly decent person sitting across from us at dinner. "His eyebrows are too close together." "Her butt is a bit wide." "He's boring." "She laughs like a hyena." "His middle is thicker than I like." "She's got a crooked bottom tooth." "He drives an old person's car." "She did not dress sexy enough." "He is losing his hair." "She is missing a toe."

I could come up with a zillion more. But you get the point. All excuses to dismiss a type of person you are not accustomed to dating, who by the way, was the person that ripped your heart out. But if you gave the guy who drives a grandpa car a chance, you might find out that you are compatible, he's intelligent, he supports you, he has reasonable expectations and lives within healthy boundaries. He might not walk around with six pack abs or a crocodile Armani belt, but he is a hell of a catch who will be a terrific, suitable, stable partner.

Just what you deserve, petal.

THERE'S A REASON IT'S CALLED VD

Yep, Valentine's Day sucks as a single person. For couples, there are romantic candlelit dinners, roses, jewelry and passion. For singles, it is the longest, most dreadful day to get through and endure. Major relief sets in when the clock strikes midnight. Then comes the feeling of gratitude that another VD has passed and you remain unscathed.

My first single Valentine's Day was not a pleasant experience. I watched some sappy movie that made me even more miserable and depressed. I polished off a large bucket of ice cream and stayed in my pajamas the entire day. The thought of my singleness spiraled out of control. Yes, my mind went there. That dark place where everything is exaggerated and dramatic. I'll never be with anyone. I'm going to be alone forever. I'm unlovable. If I choke to death eating broccoli no one will find me until my body is half eaten by maggots. I just ate a trough of ice cream and nothing fits! I'm the only one in the world who's alone! No one in the entire universe is staying home except me. Even now, I can hear the violins playing. When I was in that state of mind, nothing anyone said could get me out of it. I mean nothing. I was adamant that I was having a pity party and no one was going to stop me. Eventually I would come around, dust myself off and continue living in my singlehood.

The top 3 issues that bugged me about VD were:
1) No flowers
2) No jewelry and
3) I was lonely.

To be satisfied, I wanted to counteract these things with positive actions I could do for myself in the future. We have the power in us to make decisions that make us feel better. My sad button was triggered by the thought that everyone on earth received flowers except me. I decided to buy myself some bright, pretty, fragrant flowers. I purchased a vibrant bouquet for $5.99 at the grocery store and put them in a crystal vase on the kitchen table. Those inexpensive flowers lasted two weeks and every time I walked by them I smiled knowing that it was an awesome gesture of love to myself.

Additionally, I took advantage of a huge January clearance sale and bought myself a topaz ring at 70% off. I wrapped it immediately and gave it to myself on Feb 14th. It's perfect! How did I know? That was almost 20 years ago. Even when I wear that ring today, it is a symbol of my ability to take damn diligent care of myself.

Flowers and jewelry were helpful, but the biggest mountain I had to climb was spending the evening alone. Eating a can of soup next to my cats watching Richard Gere in his hot white uniform scoop up Paula was how I spent my first lonely VD.

The answer was simple. I needed to reach out to someone else who was lonely or hurting. I needed to be the person for someone else that I wanted someone to be for me. I understood it would not be a 'romantic' encounter, but I also recognized that asking a friend to join me for dinner or a movie would probably make her night as well as mine.

Two people who are lonely on their own are not lonely when they come together.

I incorporated these actions on any other occasion where I had the potential to be a miserable sad sack. And it worked like a charm. It worked so well that I still do it!

IT'S TIME TO LET GO AND FORGIVE

You fell madly in love at one point. Yeah, things went wrong, perhaps horribly wrong, but you are rebuilding your own life now and forgiving is the best way to move on in a positive way.

Forgiving does not mean you will let her or him off the hook for hurting you. Forgiving will help you. Forgiving assists you in setting your mind free of the pain you experienced. Forgiving does not mean forgetting, it means not letting the pain and anger consume you. Forgiveness provides freedom for you. It breaks the negative vibe you have for the other person.

This visual example helped me very much. Picture yourself walking down the street. Attached to your ankle is this large linked chain with a bowling ball at the end. You carry this around with you where ever you go. That chain and ball signify your ex. Everything your ex does even months and years after the split is something you carry around with you. It's a heavy load. It makes you tired and stressed. Yet all along, you have the power to remove your foot from the chain and let it go. Your heavy load is lifted. You are letting your ex live his/her life, and you are free to live yours. The invisible bondage has been broken. Once you forgive, their actions will not affect you. Forgiveness is a present beautifully wrapped in a blue Tiffany box that you gift yourself.

Sometimes it's excruciatingly tough to forgive. It may take time and work with a therapist or loving friend, but it's worth it when you let go.

For example, when I tried to forgive my mother, I didn't feel I had the strength to do it myself. I did not know how to forgive. I said the words out loud, but they were just words. I prayed, God, please help me forgive. I must have prayed this prayer a thousand times. Eventually I was able to forgive. I no longer carried the weight of all that anger and resentment towards her. I didn't like what happened, I did not forget what happened, but once I forgave her, we were able to have a cordial relationship with a few laughs in between. It wasn't perfect, but I was able to set boundaries to make it work.

Forgiveness is a gift you give to yourself. If you do not forgive, you will hold onto bitterness, rage and chances are you will complain and gripe and blame. When will it end?

I am reminded of a woman in her fifties who had not spoken to her brother in over ten years. He lived in another state with his wife and children. I asked her what caused the strife between them. With watery eyes she couldn't remember exactly, she just knew they didn't agree on *something...* whatever that something was. As I questioned her more about the situation, I felt like she was ripping open a wound that had been scabbed over for years, but never healed. Obviously, there was pain but it was as if she dismissed it from her mind until she was forced to deal with it. As we continued talking, she made the decision to contact him. Fast forward several months, they are in contact and trying to rebuild their connection. Such healing!

I have experienced brokenness in a close relationship and completely understand the feelings associated with it. The conviction that I was right and I will not back down, the frustration that I can't attend an event because that other person would be there, the sadness I felt because I couldn't share the happy news with that person. The thoughts I told myself: It's for the best. I don't want to fight. It's better this way. We can never get past this. I just don't want to deal with it. But life goes on. The first birthday arrives and still not speaking. No card, no cake, no call. Holidays, graduations, kid's birthday parties, anniversaries, special dinners come and go and the absence of that person becomes the new normal. My truth: Even though they were not physically there, it didn't mean I didn't want them there. I wished we could work it out. On some level. On any level. Somehow.

There are many levels of brokenness. Obviously if someone is causing you physical or emotional harm, then removing yourself from the situation is the healthy and necessary thing to do. If someone neglected to get you a glass of water and you cut them out of your life, there might be an opportunity for restoration here.

There are going to be times when people let us down. That's a fact. They might reveal your darkest secret, they might lie straight to your face, they might not put the radio station on a channel you listen to, they might criticize every move you make, they might party too much at that important event, they might try to make you feel less than, they might have unrealistic expectations, they might say cruel things behind your back, they might disagree with everything you say.

What if you decided to extend an olive branch to that person to help you move forward? A short email stating, "Hope you have a nice birthday." "Thinking of you this holiday season." Or send a whimsical card that is simple and thoughtful. Or pick up the phone and say, "Hello. I think it's time we talk." It is your choice to decide how close you want to get once a reconciliation begins. You might not want that person to go on a month-long road trip with you, but you may agree that it would be acceptable to attend the same function together.

You might suggest that you avoid heated topics that typically end up in an argument. You might agree that no smoking or drinking is allowed around your children. You might need to vent and tell your side of the story without interruption. You might need to refrain from telling this person anything personal. You might need to quietly remove yourself from an uncomfortable situation.

If you extend an olive branch and the response is positive, that's marvelous darling! But if you don't receive a pleasant response, please know you tried, you reached out and did your best to mend the situation. If someone doesn't want a relationship with me, I don't have the ability to change anyone's mind. I could pant and beg I guess, but that's rather unbecoming. Even though the outcome is not as I had hoped, there is a sense of relief and stress lifted from me after having reached out. My shoulders relax and there is closure. I can't control other people's response, but I know that because I made every effort to repair the brokenness, I can allow myself to let it go.

A reconciliation on any level can be the best action step you can make. It's time.

NOT YET

While dating, there were moments that my frustration level flew off the charts. The depressing, gloom and doom, sad-sack, hopeless gremlin on my shoulder constantly whispered in my ear: "You're never going to find anyone." "You're not pretty enough to find a man." "You expect him to move out of his mother's house at age 50, you're being too picky." "You will be alone forever, face it cupcake."

Once I fell into the victim trap, I complained and crabbed until I got the negativity out of my system and eventually mustered up the courage to get out there again. Once I dusted myself off, my hope was renewed.

Until the next disastrous blind date.

And the one who conveniently forgot to tell me that I had a huge piece of spinach in my front teeth.

And the one where I had to crawl through the driver's side window to sit in the passenger's seat.

And the one who admitted he wanted to dismember his ex-wife's boyfriend.

And the one who asked me if I was open to wearing whipped cream underwear.

I did not understand it. I whitened my teeth. I read every dating book ever written. I attached a list of qualities of my perfect man to a helium balloon and watched it float out into the universe. I was confident in my appearance. I cleaned out my rotten onion, formerly known as emotional baggage. I squirted perfume on my nether region. I went to events alone. I said yes to every invitation. I took golf lessons. I speed dated. I took a pottery class. I bought a new expensive, lift-up bra. I danced like a monkey. I developed healthy boundaries. I painted my toenails. I squeezed cantaloupe in the grocery store next to single men. I did everything in my power to put myself out there.

Still no prince charming. But plenty of toads. I had heard that finding a partner is like finding a matching sock in a gigantic pile of socks. Each sock you pick that is not a match will get you one sock closer to the right match.

The waiting game is not easy. When I want something, I want it **now.** I don't want to have to go on 40 million stupid blind dates. I don't want to have to pluck my eyebrows and shave my legs every weekend. I don't want to spend any more nights wondering when my time will come.

When I was at my wits end about *still* being single, I admit, I took my anger out on God. (Sorry God!) On my commute to work, I started in on Him. "I know You can just snap Your special God finger and have my perfect mate standing next to me at Dunkin Donuts tomorrow morning. You have the power to do that! So why don't You wiggle Your Godly nose and give me what I want? I won't ask for anything ever again. I promise!"

I was emotional and acted like a toddler having a temper tantrum. These rants of mine usually lasted an hour, conveniently the exact amount of time it took for my commute to work. Before pulling in the parking lot, I apologized to God and tried to shake off my agitation and aggravation. I also spit out my binkie before entering the building.

Then I wait a few days, a week, a month. A year. Two years. Nothing. Just another uneventful weekend or another blind date that slammed a door in my face.

When we want something so badly and it does not come, we experience all sorts of emotions. Lack of faith, frustration, depression, anger,

99

hopelessness, impatience.

It was as if life was telling me Not Yet. For me, God was telling me not yet. I didn't like it but after a while it forced me to widen my perspective on the waiting game. Maybe it was nothing I was doing or not doing. Maybe the right person simply had not crossed my path yet. Maybe our first encounter was in the works. The cougar in me thought maybe he wasn't born yet. Maybe the chess pieces were being manipulated behind the scenes to arrange the perfect match. Maybe. Maybe it was time for me to be okay on my own. Maybe it was time for me to lavish myself in self-love. Maybe I could be the best person I could be while waiting. Maybe I can be a vessel for someone who is hopeless and in need. Maybe this time alone was teaching me how to be grateful and to appreciate each day.

As I look back on the excruciatingly long waiting period before I met my husband, there definitely were positives I took away. I became stronger, more independent, more resilient, more accepting of myself. Because I had to wait and wait and wait and freaking wait, I dug deep and persevered. I humbled myself and asked for help when needed. I mustered up the courage to confront those who I felt wronged me. I had a hell of a time going out with my friends. I bought a silver bullet. I pushed myself and ventured out on my own. I tested my limitations. I opened myself up to new adventures, volunteer activities, expanded my circle of friends. I developed a huge appreciation for my male friends who supported me, helped me decorate the Christmas tree and increased my confidence. I learned to be okay staying home alone. I stopped checking under the bed for monsters.

I grew so much.

The Not Yet period became a starting point for me to build a foundation of being content and okay with being single. During the Not Yet period, I still yearned for a partner, but eventually became conscious of the fact that I could live a fulfilling, productive life in the meantime.

Now that is empowerment.

In a world of instant everything, it is tough to wait for our prayers to be answered. Very tough. I know I expected God to give me my soul mate the Monday after my divorce, but no one appeared. If I could have sculpted him out of play dough, I would have, but God had other plans.

During times of major frustration, I started to reason why I was still single. This got me in trouble. I went there. I convinced myself it was my fault. I said to myself, "I must not be _____ enough." (fill in the blank); Pretty, perky, smoldering, cultured, captivating, educated. And worst of all, I must not be *good* enough. The worst gremlin of all!

When we convince ourselves of these untrue thoughts, we might settle for someone who does not treat us right. We might use our sexuality to lure someone into a commitment. We might shut down and not open ourselves up to love – thinking that love will never come anyway so why bother? We might sabotage any chance of a decent start with someone because of this negative, untrue self-talk.

When I feel this way, this is the time for a very necessary pep talk. I need to convince myself that I am perfectly okay. I just have not met the right person. Simple as that. I will wait for the person I am meant to be with. The one I am in tune with. The one who respects and adores me.

In the meantime, I will live each day saying yes to new experiences, thinking positive thoughts about myself, laughing my butt off and tending to my own needs.

As far as meeting my soul mate? It's not time. Not yet.

Yeah, Nope, not yet.

No. Not yet.

101

And then suddenly, someone special pops out of nowhere and rocks your world!!

BELIEVE

Beliefs manifest change.

It is critical to believe your life can be transformed.

Believe that you can make minor adjustments and over time, you will start to feel better. Move an inch at a time. Dip your toe in the newness of an extraordinary adventure!

Believe that you can have an amazing future even though you had a rotten, abusive, sucky, painful past. It will take an open heart, willingness and commitment from you, but it is achievable. Your past is just one block of time in your life. Your future is another block of time. Don't let your past ruin your future.

Believe you can make healthy choices. You may not have felt you had a choice in the past, but now you can make wise decisions. Eat an apple, walk away, let petty things go, master the downward dog, stand up for yourself.

Believe you have a worthy purpose. Your life has significant meaning. You were created for a higher purpose. Now go out and discover what that is! And if you know what it is, take time to develop it and spread it around for others to benefit!

Believe that you are special even though other people might not have told you so. Others may not have treated you like the incredible person you are. We are all God's children. And God did not make junk. Acknowledge every single one of your strengths and talents and be a bright light for others. You are extraordinary, unique and fabulous *just the way you are*.

Believe that surrounding yourself with supportive people is critical to improving your life. Maybe there are toxic people around you. You

103

have the choice to detach from them (with grace) and develop bonds with encouraging, uplifting people who will build you up and not tear you down. Their positive belief in you will begin to rub off on you.

Believe that as an adult you can make your own decisions, even if you were not able to as a young person. As a child, you may have been seen but not heard. Your thoughts might not have counted for much, or anything at all. Now as an adult, you can make impactful choices for yourself. You have a strong voice and the power and ability to choose wisely.

Believe that life will give you a second chance...and a third... and a fourth. You might think that one mistake can destroy your plan and it's all over. Fortunately, life goes on and we can redeem ourselves. It might take time, but we can try and try and try until we get it right. Believe you can begin again. And again. And again.

Believe that if you want something, you need to be it first. If you want love, give love. If you want respect, give respect. If you want peace, be peaceful. You might think this is backwards, but trust me, it is the way to bring blessings to your life. People yearn to be around those who are loving, giving, respectful. The more you release your beautiful heart; the more people will gravitate toward you.

Believe that you have the strength to release yourself from those that are not showing you appreciation. If someone is not treating you right, you might fear that you absolutely cannot detach from them. Somehow you owe them or will feel guilty if you walk away. But you know in your gut that you need to be apart. It might be an uncomfortable adjustment for you at first, but you are doing the right thing for yourself by detaching.

Believe that you deserve love. Why? Because you do. Simple as that. You might think that you are not worthy of being cherished. Other people deserve love because they are prettier or smarter. That is an untruth. You deserve love just as all of us deserve love.

Believe that you are capable of setting boundaries. You do not have to accept behavior that is inappropriate. We might feel if we set a boundary that someone will leave us. We fear abandonment. But we know that we are not being treated the way we should be. Setting boundaries is necessary for our self-esteem. It means that you will not accept unfair or negative behavior. Boundary setting might be hard at first, but you will feel stronger and more confident the more you do it.

Believe that you can take care of yourself while in a partnership. All your energy goes to the spouse or the kids. There is no time for yourself. You are exhausted. But you have the choice to say, tonight I'm going to enjoy a night out with friends, or I'm going for a massage. The other family members might be taken off guard at first, but they can handle things for a few hours. You can make this choice. We all need to refuel and replenish ourselves.

Believe you are worthy of good things. Yes, you. You are worthy. You don't have to be rich, privileged, tall, blue-eyed, educated, or intelligent to receive the blessings life has to offer. You are worthy just as you are – warts, cellulite, wrinkles and all. Whether you are crabby, depressed, volatile, uneducated, spoiled, disabled, chubby, alcoholic, stubborn, snobby, ignorant, you name it – you are worthy of greatness.

Believe that you are God's child and are special. You are strong. You are magnificent. You are capable. You are unique and special in your own right. You have traits like no one else.

Believe that you bring compelling conversations, ideas, thoughts, creativity, and wonder like no one else in the world. You are like a snowflake - authentic and magical.

Believe that you are talented wherever your passion lies. You may grow a whopper of a tomato, carve a cartoon character out of a tree stump, or determine the kind of wine you're about to taste with just a sniff. You can walk across a tightrope, fly a plane upside down, or make the most amazing tartar sauce ever. Talents are everywhere! Use those gifts to entertain, educate, and enhance someone's life. Don't let them go to waste. Others need what you have to offer.

Believe that once you get through the storm, there will be relief. Storms do not last forever. Sometimes they teach us lessons, help us go deeper or show us that we have others to lean on. Storms are no picnic, but afterwards (and it *will* end), you will have peace. You are strong enough to endure difficult obstacles. Remember, rainbows appear after a storm, not before.

Believe if you commit to yourself, your life will shift. Things don't happen overnight. We all want drive-through break-throughs but transformation takes commitment, determination, healthy decisions, endurance and time. That breakthrough will not happen overnight, but if you are determined to stay the course, you will see results. Remind yourself that there will be a light at the end of the tunnel and it will be far better than what you had imagined.

Believe you can love again. If you have been hurt, it could be your choice to armor yourself and block off your heart even though you crave a relationship. No dating, no venturing out. You might sabotage any chance of meeting a new potential mate because the fear of getting hurt again is too great. But as you grow and begin to trust yourself during the healing period, you can slowly become open to love again.

Believe not everyone will hurt you. We might close ourselves off from intimacy because we experienced pain, rejection, abuse, hurt. The thing is, not everyone will cause you pain or reject you. Not everyone is the same. Not everyone will hurt you. Trust your instincts.

Believe you are not responsible for other people's issues. Just because someone is in a bad mood and takes it out on you, does not mean you have to take it on. You are not the reason it's thundering outside.

Believe in the power of friendships. Value your friends whether you are single or not. Your friends are with you for the long haul, through ups and downs, crazy wild times, breakups, and everything else in between. Lifelong friendships are irreplaceable and worth nurturing.

Believe your voice matters. You may have been shut down, ignored, not heard, felt invisible for many years. But your adventures, experiences, conversations and wisdom have value. Your voice is confident and inspiring. People are interested to hear what you have to say. Many will learn from your experiences.

Believe you don't have to settle. Somewhere deep down you feel the situation you are in is not right. You want more. You make the choice to leave the mediocre situation and reach for the stars. You deserve the best and you wait for something better to come along. Or better yet, you take the steps to create something better.

Believe you can be a huge blessing in someone's life. So many ways to help people! Make a game out of it. Who can I bless today? What can I do to give hope to someone? When you start giving for the sake of giving and not for the sake of getting back, your whole existence will change.

Believe that when you release something that does not feel right, you are allowing space for something better to come in.

Believe you can live on your own and take care of yourself while dating. You have the skills to depend on yourself.

Believe you have the power to say no. If something does not feel right, you have every right to say no.

Believe you can thrive and soar! Why? Because you can!

Believe you can love yourself enough to give up a struggle over something you have no control over.

GAYLE'S DATING THOUGHTS

This chapter represents my view on various issues where one might get stuck. These are my female opinions only. Agree or disagree, but these nuggets of wisdom guided me during the rollercoaster ride of dating.

Dare Not Compare!

Comparing ourselves to others is dangerous territory. We usually compare ourselves to those we think have something more worthwhile than we do. Comparisons come from our idea that we are lacking and others have an abundance. Oh, her lips are full and plump, mine are thin and wormlike. Her friends are cool and fashionable, mine are nerds and drab. Her butt is round and perfect, mine is as flat as a pancake. She is smarter than me, prettier than me, more creative than me, a better salsa dancer than me, she doesn't get pimples, she doesn't have as much hair on her arms, her skin is smoother.

Comparisons could go to infinity and beyond. Bottom line, there will *always* be someone that has better, bigger, fancier, superior, perkier, snazzier, and more exceptional. This is a fact. And whether we verbalize it or obsess in our head, comparing does us no good. Zip. Nada. Zilch.

The grass may appear greener, and it may very well be, but comparing will not help you in your quest to grow a bigger cucumber, find your prince charming, or have a smaller bone structure. Spending precious time continually yearning for what someone else has will lead to disappointment because your focus is on what you don't have rather than being grateful for what you do have.

Appreciate your intellect, your crazy personality, your spot-on cooking abilities, the way you make others feel at ease, your instinctive parenting skills, your devotion to animals. You are born with blessings galore. What may be strange to you is that the person you think has it all, may be looking at you and wishing she had your hysterical sense of humor or perfectly chiseled forearms.

You don't need to compare yourself to anyone else. You have all you need. Appreciate your individuality because there is no one in the world like you. And that, twinkle toes, makes you one in a million.

<u>You can allow someone to get close. Trust your gut.</u>

After a painful breakup or an abusive childhood, we might dress ourselves in a coat of armor or bubble wrap so no one will ever get near our heart. We keep our distance, are cordial, but will not let anyone in again. Our heart was ripped open once, it ain't never gonna happen again!

We might convince ourselves that *not* being with a mate is what we really want, when deep down inside we yearn for someone to share our life with. But the idea of potentially getting crushed again is not something we are willing to entertain. I'm not implying that everyone who is not in a relationship wants to be in one, but there are those who remain single because the pain of being vulnerable is too much to bear.

I had this same fear. I was petrified to put myself out there. The shield that protected my heart was 15 feet thick. I flirted and flirted some more, but if anyone attempted to get too close, up went the armor. But over time, I began to trust my instincts. There was no guarantee that I would never be hurt again, but my intuition told me when to give someone a try and when to walk away.

I can meet someone, take infant steps, keep it flowing at my pace. If I see red flags, I will proceed with caution or release him from my life. If there are no flags, I'll take another teeny weenie step. I will trust that not everyone will hurt me.

<u>If someone tells you they don't want to commit, believe them.</u>

Heartbreak often happens when we try to stick our round peg into his square hole. If someone is crystal clear and says they are not interested in getting married or being in a committed relationship, assume they are telling the truth. So often (and I am guilty of this) we think *we* are the one who can change his mind. I guess it does happen, but I've only seen it on a make-believe movie.

If you want a committed partnership, it is not with this person. If it quacks like a duck and walks like a duck, it's not a husband. No matter what you do, you won't change him. He is the only one in control of that and he has made it perfectly clear that he does not want to be a Mr. Right.

<u>If you have to lie and live in secret to be in this relationship, it is not the best decision.</u>

I'm not referring to keeping your newfound love private for a while once you get to know if he could be a potential keeper. I'm referring to dating someone who asks you to climb out of the upstairs bathroom window and walk three flights down the fire escape wearing a dark hoodie when leaving his apartment. Or he repeatedly tells you he will leave his dreadful wife but never seems to make a move.

Save yourself some time and a tubful of tears and seek out someone who wants to shout out to the world that his incredible girlfriend is walking out his front door! You are a complete woman, you don't have to settle for a half of a relationship.

<u>Just because a man likes me as a girlfriend, doesn't mean I am obligated to like him as a boyfriend.</u>

As a young girl, I wanted a boy to love me. I was not the type of girl who had a line of boys knocking down my door. So, when someone did form a solo line I thought I was supposed to like him back. Even as a big girl adult, I believed the same thing. If there was interest, I better latch onto him like a leech because another one might never come along. Dating in my 30's was challenging enough, but with this mindset, I would now be married to the man who confessed his love to me on a blind date while I was chewing on a cherry tomato.

It truly pained me when I met a nice man who wanted to date me and I wasn't feeling it. I told myself I should continue dating him even though my romantic feelings were non-existent. Not even after a few cocktails. But I was reminded of the promise I made to myself. And that was to be honest, be who I am, and make decisions that serve my highest good and my truth. Pretending I was feeling something I was not was not the right move for either of us.

Regardless if the right one comes along, this lesson meant freedom to me.

<u>Surround yourself with honest, positive, healthy people.</u>

Having genuine, solid, compassionate, uplifting, loving people around us will help us reach a higher level.

During my divorce I would call my step mother at 1 am when I was sad, I'd cry to my father because I had to mow the lawn, my friends and sister were rocks for me. I could not have sanely pressed through without every single supportive person by my side. When I fell, they were there. They looked beyond my faults and believed in me. There is no better gift on earth than when someone sees and wants the absolute best for you. These folks are keepers. I am beyond blessed.

Stepping Out In Love

<u>Allow yourself to be wooed!</u>

I can only speak from my perspective, but I feel a woman should be courted. Old school or not, I believe the man should initially pursue the woman, and the woman be open and receptive if she is interested. Oh, flirt and be silly, but when a man wants to go out with you, he will find a way and take the lead.

You might be rolling your eyes thinking, "Gayle, this is not 1950, if I want someone I'm going after him. I have no problem asking him out." And I get that, but I think when a man and woman start to date, it's nice when the man takes the initiative and plans the dinner and activities.

It's like the hunter gatherer concept. I believe women are the gift. And I believe men will pursue a woman he wants.

Being an independent, strong woman, it was challenging to sit back and allow myself to be courted, but I forced myself to refrain from emailing first, not plan the entire evening, or be the first to plan the next date.

Woo eventually fades, so I relaxed and savored the short-lived woo.

<u>Maintain friendships, regardless.</u>

It is common for people to spend less time with friends once they become a couple. Yes, it will happen that you will spend more time with the boyfriend, but always, always nourish and maintain your friendships.

Romantic interests might come and go but loyal friends are like another arm, they will remain with you for the long haul. Even if you are in a paired up and your friend is not, you can still hang, cackle until you cry, and do crazy stuff only girlfriends do.

Quality friends are for keeps. Carve out time for them. You won't be sorry. Most of the time I have spit out my drink laughing was due to my friend cracking me up. Enough said.

Find Time to Date.

You want to date but make excuses that you are too busy, too tired, don't feel like it, and just can't make it work. If you want to date, find a way. Even if it's meeting for an appetizer for an hour, it's good to have some 'me' time and interesting conversation. You deserve it. Turn off the TV, get up an hour earlier to do your household chores, and carve out a few hours to date that nice guy at work.

Fill your life with activities that knock your socks off!

In other words, don't sit on top of the phone waiting for that hunky guy to call. Or text. Or beep. Or blip. Develop hobbies that give you pleasure and occupy your time. Garden, hula hoop, yoga, jump out of a plane, join a bowling or pool league, sing, play the harp, sew some curtains.

Getting involved with various activities will help you develop a confident sense of self, create a life you love and will make you so desirable! You will fill your time with activities that you treasure and it will enhance the quality of your single life.

What will happen is you will become more comfortable in your own skin. Your newfound passions will certainly fill a void in your life. During the process of developing hobbies, you might meet other interesting folks that you connect with on a deeper level. Who knows? You might meet a new lifetime friend! The sky is the limit. Point is, these new skills and activities that you are engaging in will enhance your life.

So, when he calls while you are doing all this cool stuff, you will call him back when you are free. He sees you living a full and vibrant life...and he wants to be part of it.

<u>Stay present.</u>

I'll be happy when I'm not alone; when I'm single; when I'm pregnant; when the kids leave for college; when he stays home; when he goes out. This way of thinking keeps us in an anxious state of mind.

The secret is to accept and thrive where we are on the way to where we are going. Strive towards reaching your goals but embrace the now! Today is all we have, tomorrow is never guaranteed. Not to be a Debby-downer, but it's true.

Get off your phone and be present. Look your children in the eye. Be in the moment. Relish the gifts life is offering you right now. The things you yearn for might not be what they are cracked up to be.

<u>If you're constantly questioning yourself, it might not be the right fit.</u>

My belief is that when it's the right union, it will be effortless and easy. Conversations will flow and both parties will be respected. No uncertainty. No questioning. When he says he will call, he will call. Easy.

There are times when we date someone and feel like we are walking on eggshells. We think we said something inappropriate because we get mixed messages. We think he is aloof because of something we did or didn't do. Always questioning if we did something wrong and feeling badly about ourselves.

The healthiest relationship is when communication is clear and we know exactly where we stand. If it's great one day and awful the next, then great again, then awful once again, it might be time to reassess. And if after discussions your questions are not answered, maybe this is not the best fit for you.

These tips were instrumental in increasing my confidence and self-assuredness. Most important, be with the one who lifts you up, cherishes and respects you and accepts you as you are, warts and all.

REJECTION? DUMPED? NAH.

My first date after my divorce was with a handsome man whom I met on match.com. We laughed and talked about ourselves, work, life, kids, goals, what we wanted in life. It seemed like we had known each other for a lifetime. As we winded down, with no prompting of my own, he asked for my number and said he wanted to see me again. He kissed me on the cheek and said he'd call soon.

As I drove home, the evening replayed in my mind. Great eye contact, nice back and forth talking, no dull awkward moments, a little flirting on his part, a little giggling on mine. He touched my arm and leg a few times. We had goofy and serious moments. It was a perfect meeting. When I arrived home, I sent him a charming thank you email (after all he did pick up the tab for the drinks and appetizers).

After I forwarded my delightful, slightly manipulative email, within a few seconds, his name popped up on my screen. He replied so fast, he must have been waiting to hear from me!

"Nice to meet you but I'm not interested in you."

What? I read it again...*not interested in you...*

Rejection?

A few short hours ago he said he liked me, he told me he had fun, he laughed with me, he shared personal things about himself, he flirted, he asked for my number, he said he wanted to see me again. These things he said were not coerced by me, they were *his* words, and he said them without hesitation.

I felt the tears well up quickly. That little tickle in my nose before it turns bright red and the flood gates opened.

What was wrong with me? Why didn't he like me? Did I turn him off? Was my cleavage not showing enough? Was I boring? Should I have had sex with him behind the bar? Why am I such a loser? Poor me! No one will ever love me!

After not having an answer to these berating questions, I drifted back in time. I was 13, in 8th grade and came home after a special dance. I had put on a little makeup, wore a lovely dress, and felt pretty before I left. I was excited to go. I tried to be brave when I came home, but everyone could tell that it didn't go well. I was heartbroken when no one asked me to slow dance. I walked head-down past my family and blubbered up the stairs to my room before I shut the door to release my pain in private. Dealing with hurt on my own was something I was accustomed to dealing with on my own, or with my dog Mike.

Much to my surprise, after a few hearty sobs into my pillow, there was a knock on my bedroom door. It was my mother. She rarely, if ever, came to my room when I was upset. She basically kept her distance until I got over whatever it was that hurt me. Consoling me wasn't in her comfort zone or maybe she didn't know how to deal with me. I also think that she didn't like that I was weak. I'm not sure about that, but my gut felt it loudly.

I was vulnerable when I opened my bedroom door, yet I welcomed and yearned for any advice or support. I do remember feeling happy she took the time to talk to me. She knew this night meant a lot to me. She remained standing and looked me straight in the eye and said, "I don't understand why no one asked you to dance Gayle. It must be something that you are doing to make them not want to dance with you."

That statement has haunted me for years. When I dated my ex, Ma pulled him aside and asked him, "So, what is so special about Gayle that you want to date her?" I don't know about anyone else, but to me that question was asking him, "Why the hell would you want to date *her*?" My interpretation, it might not have been what she meant. But that's what I felt.

Because my mother told me that there was something wrong with me, I believed it. Being told something like this by the person who brought me into this world and who was supposed to love me unconditionally, cut me to the bone. I believed this statement to be truth, just like my eyes are blue and I have two legs. Once I received the email from this dude, those words spoken to me that night in my bedroom 22 years prior came rushing back into my brain. And it hurt.

After a few hours of this head torture, I quieted myself and thought through his response a bit more. I'd spent an enormous amount of energy improving my self-esteem. I grew leaps and bounds and learned to love myself and treat myself with thoughtfulness and consideration. These questions I asked myself were not in my best interest. They were hurting me.

I could have ripped him a new one and blamed him for my insecurities and bright red nose, but that was not the right thing to do.

I pondered my last years and how proud I was of myself. I've grown into an independent and self-assured woman. I was determined that this man that I spent only a few hours with was **_not_** going to make me feel like crap about myself. I was done with that – or at least trying to be done with that. I was so tired of putting myself down because someone else dissed me.

I decided to make a list of my truths. These truths helped me bounce back from this rejection.

The way Joe handled the situation was on him, not me. Truth is he had no intention of seeing me again. And honestly, that was okay. I don't know what his intentions were for telling me he wanted to see me again. I don't know and it's not my business. The reasoning for his misrepresentation had nothing to do with me. Period.

119

I can go on a blind date and have a fabulous evening! I don't have to marry my date or even see him again. If I can live in the moment without expectations of a happily ever after outcome, that is a healthy experience. I can honestly say that I can hold my own and I am proud of that.

Just because one man was not interested in pursuing me does not mean I will never find the right person.

Even though one person does not find me attractive, doesn't mean I am not attractive. I have male friends who are amazing human beings, but I don't find them attractive. That doesn't mean they aren't nice, or an awesome catch, or that they wouldn't be attractive to someone else. I thought long and hard about this. For someone who doesn't find me attractive, it just means for that one person I am not a match. Doesn't mean I'm a loser or a birdbrain. This was pivotal for my self-esteem.

I'm not going to give the guy all my power. I was happy after the date because *I thought he thought* I was funny. Was he the right fit for me? Hmmm?? I don't think so.

I was so concerned about what he thought of me that I really did not acknowledge how he made *me* feel. I was so focused on how good looking he was that I didn't really zone in on what he, as a potential partner, offered me. I am the interviewer and it's up to me to discover the kind of man that is right for me.

Most importantly, because a date did not work out, it did not mean there was something wrong with me. It did not mean there was something wrong with him.

Our pairing simply was not a match.

That simple sentence changed my entire perspective on dating and relationships, job interviews, house hunting, friendships.

BAHAMA MAMAS AND CRUISE CHICKS

Two of my closest friends, Kellie and Irene, divorced around the same time I did. I was not happy when they split, but I was grateful to have best friends who could completely relate to the misery of a split. We all understood. We were all in the same place. We just knew.

What better way to bond with friends than to go on a post-divorce vacation? We decided to go to the Bahamas for a four-day getaway. The price was right. The timing was right. The decision was right. Our mindset was right.

Once we landed and arrived at The Atlantis and looked up at the amazing structure in front of us, we knew we did the right thing. We dropped off our luggage in the room and made a bee line to the pool.

For four days we vegged by the pool, drank an obnoxious amount of alcohol and were entertained by Sven, who was in charge of fluffing our lounge pillows. We were drained, deflated, emotionally spent, physically exhausted, and uncertain of our futures. We were horizontal the entire time on the comfy cushioned loungers and were unapologetic. We had survived an emotional roller coaster, and this was a gift we gave ourselves. Sun, Sleep, Sven, and Strawberry Daquiris.

There was a connectedness between us like I've never experienced before. Beaten down from tirelessly trying to make our marriages work and now finding ourselves wondering where life will take us. We understood each other without having to say a word.

It was a tremendous getaway and by the end of the trip, we felt understood and ready to press on. Thank goodness we were smart enough to bring peanut butter and crackers, because we couldn't afford to eat there.

Stepping Out In Love

A few years later…

My dear friend Diane asked me if I wanted to go on a cruise to France and Italy with her and 6 other single women. Each of us knew only one or two of the other girls, but no one knew everyone. It had the potential to be a disaster – yet was anything but.

Diane and I arrived in Spain a day before the departure date. Ola and el bonya was the extent of my Spanish. We quickly figured out what Sangria was and only stopped at restaurants with pictured menus where we could point at eggs, potatoes and bread. We met up with our new traveling buddies and soon after embarked on a weeklong European vacation. Right out of the gate I was impressed with the girls. They were independent, intelligent, worldly, savvy, professional and loads of fun!

On day one of the cruise we all met for happy hour. We were a schmorg of hairspray and eye liner waiting to tear up Europe. When seated for dinner, we were intentionally and strategically placed next to the Captains table. Eight women who commanded attention received just that - free bottles of booze, specialty desserts and a special invitation by the captain himself to visit the bridge of the ship. One of my new friends was serenaded by a slew of handsome waiters for her fake happy birthday!

One morning we docked in Nice, France. On some excursions we split up but this was a special day where we planned to check out folks in their birthday suits sunbathing on the French Riviera. I had no desire to expose myself, but a couple of my newbie friends had the guts to set their puppies free. Karen, quite impressive! Looking down at my droopy old dogs, I'm glad I remained covered. After witnessing many naked walkers who looked worse than I did, I decided to go shopping. The beach and the shops were near the dock so I was comfortable exploring on my own. After spending a fortune on French clothes and accessories, I ran into one of the singing waiters.

"Hello!" he said with a big smile. "You're one of the eight single women?" Guess we hit celebrity status.

"Yes, and you're one of our singing waiters!" I big-smiled right back.

"Yes!" He winked. "Would you like to have a drink?"

Handsome, spoke several languages, age-appropriate, good singing voice. We had a drink in a small outdoor café overlooking the ocean. To say it was picturesque would be an understatement. He asked if he could visit me in my cabin after his shift ended. He liked my blond hair and that I had some meat on me. He said the women in France were too skinny for his taste. That was the first time I was ahead in the skinny vs. meaty race. After 9 minutes of conversation, I gave him my cabin number. Totally uncharacteristic of me.

Since I had not been in a relationship for more than five years, the idea that I was still a female was uncertain. I joked that I was androgynous, like Pat on Saturday Night Live. I shut down my feminine side. I went to work, was a good mom and hung out with a ton of friends, but completely put a wall up when it came to intimacy.

I wasn't stupid. I was well-aware of what was about to happen. There was something strangely empowering about it though. I was calling the shots in some weird way. It was time to get back in touch with the fact that I *was* a woman and it was okay to desire and be desired. Five years without a touch (except for my masseuse, who I had to pay!), five years without a cuddle and five years not knowing if I would ever be intimate with a man again. I was empowered because it was _my_ decision, there were no strings, and after all, I had to find out if it actually was like riding a bike, like they all say.

To calm my nerves, I downed a few shots of vodka prior to the knock on my door. The sock that hung on the doorknob alerted Diane to sleep across the hall. All I will say about our encounter is that I thoroughly enjoyed being contorted into a wheelbarrow.

Something clicked for me on that cruise. It finally penetrated through my thick skull that there was life after divorce. I became ready to trust my instinct and see if someone out there was right for me. I was open to the possibility of finding love. I was open for the right man to enter my life. That man was not the singing waiter, but he certainly helped increase my confidence and open my heart.

Instead of singing "I'm The King of the World" at the bow of the ship I wanted to shout out, "I am Woman. Hear Me Roar!"

TAKE YOURSELF ON A DATE!

In between working on my emotional health, going on miserable first dates and being agonizingly lonely, I dreamed of being asked these questions:

Gayle, would you like to:
- Take a drive to Maine and get a bowl of lobster bisque?
- See the Phantom of the Opera at the Wang Center?
- Relax with a hot stone massage at your favorite spa?
- Dine at that new Asian fusion restaurant in the city?
- Receive gorgeous fragrant flowers?
- Attend an art gallery opening?
- Take a joy ride to a random beach and soak in the sun?

YES, to all!

You're single and you find yourself giving these excuses:

- I would go, but I can't find anyone to go with me.
- All my friends are coupled-up and I don't want to be the third wheel.
- I'm too scared to attend by myself.
- I don't know anyone there and no one is available to be my plus one.
- I really want to go, but everyone I asked is busy.
- Everyone will think I'm a loser if I go solo.
- Oh gee, there are going to be many couples there, I could not possibly go by myself.

Any of these statements sound familiar? Yeah, all of these are generic excuses to keep us in the box and not go out of our comfort zone. We can always say we're not comfortable going alone, so therefore it's not going to happen.

By saying this, you will miss out on so much. What if you responded this way instead?

- I might not be so comfortable going alone, but it will force me to talk to people I otherwise would not have talked to.

- If my friend came with me, I'd be engaging only with her and would not have met all these interesting people tonight!

- I guess going solo will force me out of my shell. I am totally capable of saying hello to a stranger. I can smile and ask them what they do for a living.

- I feel empowered going to that event on my own. Turned out I did have an enjoyable evening and I connected with a single woman who I am going to have lunch with!

So, simple-minded me rationalized that I had to wait for a man to invite me to do stuff. It never occurred to me that I had the magic slippers all along. All I had to do was click three times, pull up my big girl pants, get in the car and go. The power, and the willingness, was in me.

When that lightbulb went off it was like I was living a new life. Sure, it would be awesome to have a loving partner or an available friend to do things with, but unless I bought a blow-up doll, I was on my own. So why should I neglect feeding my soul just because I happened to be single?

By declining events, I would be punishing myself by not participating in events that give me joy. I can certainly buy myself a bunch of amazing flowers. They would not smell more fragrant if someone with testicles bought them for me. The deer that I yearned to feed would not snub his nose at the corn kernels in my hand because I did not bring a date (unless the date spreads peanut butter on his palms – then I might have a problem...)

Go ahead, ask yourself on a date and go to the places you yearn to go. Don't forget to tell yourself what a fabulous time you had!

THE LIST

Like any delectable dish, you need to make a list of all the ingredients you need for that favorite recipe. You mix it all together, taste test along the way, add more salt and spice, let it simmer and voila, a deliciously crafted meal is served.

It might not be the perfect meal for everyone, but it is perfect for your individual taste.

When you are ready to buy a home, you prepare a specific list of the necessary things you must have in the house. e.g., three bedrooms, two bathrooms, open concept, nice yard. Then there are the nice-to-haves; e.g., fireplace, finished basement, screened in porch; laundry on the first floor. Then there are the deal breakers: Faulty heating system, loads of carpenter ants, house smells like dead people, two feet of water in the basement.

As you house hunt, you will weigh the pros and cons of each property. You might have to visit many houses until you find the right one. Maybe you'll have to expand your search and look in different towns. Perhaps if you look past the exterior of the house, you may see a warm, cozy place that could be perfect. And when you find it, there will be no doubt. You will pick the house that serves your needs in the best way possible.

Next list is a recipe for a man, not a pot roast.

If you do not like that he doesn't replace the paper towel roll, you might want to eliminate him. (Not from the face of the earth, just from your list).

Joking aside, it was critical to be crystal clear on the qualities I wanted in a partner, and equally important to be clear on what I did not want.

128

I literally made three columns. My list went something like this:

Must have: Good heart, trustworthy, dependable, accepts me as I am, decent job, high morals, solid, even keeled, great bear hugs, stable, has a car, (Not showing up in an uber for a date) loyal.

Nice to have: Boyish looks, funny, enjoys traveling, does not live with his parents, lots in common, taller than me, has money, has his own hair, owns own home, another home in the Caribbean.

Nope. No way. Deal breaker: Liar, violent temper, unkempt, still pining for his ex, married, mean, earful of hair, ignorant.

Once I was serious and completed my list, I burned it. That was a symbol that I was willing to let it go into the universe. My wishes rose up with the flames and I turned it over to God to make magic happen.

It might sound absolutely nuts to some people, but guess what? When I met my husband John, he had everything on the Must Have and Nice to Have list. I mean everything. In hindsight, had I known this was really going to work, I would have added that he likes to wash dishes on the must have list.

If you are yearning for love, try it. You have nothing to lose and everything to gain!

LOVE LESSONS

The person who ends up with Becca is extremely fortunate. I told her she should be treated like a gift, because she is so special. And for her to expect nothing less. Another piece of advice I gave her was to kiss a lot of boys. Only physically go where you are comfortable and always respect yourself. Take after your mommy and kiss away. And always, always remember you are the gift.

+++

I was 16 when I was asked out on my first car date. Eric was 17. He was seriously hot and I honestly couldn't believe he wanted to go out with me. On the date, I wore a pink fuzzy tight sweater, a pair of snug Jordache jeans and of course, my sexy high heeled sandals. We played kissy face at a dance a few months prior and were comfortable with each other as friends. He made reservations at a schmancy Italian restaurant where the menu displayed food in another language. There were no pictures on the menu. We each had fake ID's and went through several bottles of wine before, during and after dinner. Once we polished off the first bottle, we started to bicker about stupid things. We couldn't agree on anything and just gave each other digs. As each glass of wine emptied, the comments became more and more harsh. We nitpicked about everything and couldn't find a pleasant topic.

It was a disaster.

I found him snappy and sarcastic and ready for a fight. I'm sure the wine had something to do with our lack of chemistry, but all I could think about was how incredibly hot he was. He dropped me off at home and we kept bickering. He said some things to me before he left that were hurtful and unnecessary.

But I still wanted to go steady with him. And marry him. And have babies with him.

At this point you might think that anyone with a shred of dignity would have just dusted herself off and moved on.

Oh no, not this silly, naïve, young twinkle toes. I literally expected him to call and ask me out again. Does the word delusional mean anything to you?

Silence. I didn't hear from him. So, on Sunday morning, I decided to drive to his work and appear before him. Once he sees me he'll remember my tight, pink, fuzzy sweater and want to make out again. I parked and entered the store. I searched up and down the aisles and finally walked up to him – his back toward me. I tapped him on the shoulder.

"Hi. That was fun the other night. Wanna go out again?" (I'm cringing as I write this…)

He said, and I am not paraphrasing. These are his exact sensuous words.

'Whatever." And I watched him walk away.

BONK! That's the sound of a large, imaginary hammer pounding down on my big head.

If I had Harry Potter's magic wand, I would have turned back time. Four words worth of time. I went with my emotions and not with my gut. I didn't think of myself as a gift.

Humiliation and embarrassment have a way of teaching us what to never, ever do again. At the ripe old age 16, I learned that lesson the hard way.

On a positive note, we became friends again and both moved on.

131

About a year later, I started hanging out with a huge group of friends that worked with my best friend. About 15 of us would drink beer in the parking lot, play cards, go to the movies, and chill at each other's houses. I was good friends with Jim and one night he kissed me on the dance floor at his Christmas party. He was well mannered, delightful, tall and handsome and we had nice chemistry. Over time, the kissing happened more frequently. But a pattern starting to happen. After we stopped eating each other's faces, we would be flirty that night but the next time I saw him, he became distant. Not mean or rude, just cool. A few days or so later, we'd lock lips again and then distance. This went on for months. I still didn't understand the gift concept yet so I rolled with it.

Had I thought of myself as the gift, the second time I felt distance, we would have had a talk and no more smooching. I deserved more than that. But I hadn't learned that lesson yet. I sensed another hammer coming.

Months passed of the same hot and cold behavior. One weekend, the entire gang planned a beach weekend. Jim and I were the only two staying on Friday night and everyone else would meet us on Saturday. I had no idea what to expect but hoped for the best.

Thankfully, he was in a playful mood and asked me to go to the beach with him. I sat down on the sand and buried my bare feet in the warm sand. He started saying how much he liked me and he was sorry for being so hot and cold all these months. Acknowledgment and validation, this is a good start. Go on... He told me he loved being with me. He liked how easy I was to talk to. He wanted us to be a couple.

I was honest (yah for me) and said that I didn't understand how he could be so into me some days and standoffish on other days. (I didn't tell him that I thought his ignoring me was somehow a result of my actions...or inactions). Jim acknowledged his behavior and apologized several times. He sincerely said it will not happen again. He grabbed my hand, said something complimentary and kissed me. It was dark now and at the other end of the beach the sky lit up with brilliant fireworks. I fell for it, hook line and sinker, and was open to see where this would go. And yeah! I have a boyfriend who wants to kiss me and who will never be emotionally distant again!

The rest of the crew arrived the next day. There was so much havoc in the room that I didn't really talk to Jim while everyone was getting settled. We were all hanging out goofing around in the room. I was looking forward to spending time with Jim later but it was nice to have everyone around too. Life was good.

A few hours later, I asked Jim where he wanted to go for dinner. No eye contact. Mumbled answer. The next few hours…distance.

Are you kidding me? I was pissed. *So* pissed. After dinner, I asked my bestie to go out on the town. I looked awesome in my cool black hat and skinny jeans. He knew I was upset, but I did not give a tiny, minuscule hoot. My friend and I flirted on the boardwalk with boys, vented about how wishy-washy Jim was, and as usual, had a blast together. We got back to the room after 3 am. Jim was waiting up for me. He was syrupy sweet and I was not having it. I did not respond.

The gang didn't get together until several weeks later when Brad asked us to come over for a cookout. I knew Jim would be there but I'll be damned if he was going to stop me from hanging out with my friends. I decided ahead of time that I would be cordial, but that was all.

Jim and I did not speak until later in the evening. Jim was wasted. He was slurring his words and his big brown eyes were half shut. He was a guy that was usually in control so seeing him incoherent was out of character. He sat next to me by the bonfire.

"Hi Gayle. I'm so sorry about the way I treated you."

"Okay Jim." I said. Talk to the hand.

133

He continued on, "The thing is… uh…I'm not sure, uh, if I'm more, uh, attracted to you or, uh, to Brad.

There was the answer. An answer I really couldn't get mad at, but it explained everything. After that exchange, I learned how to be the gift.

GOLD STARS

Reluctantly, I joined match.com and literally had fifty first dates. I have a high tolerance for pain, yet many sent me searching for shots of vodka. Among them:

- the guy who yapped about himself all night, asked if I would wear whipped cream underwear, did drugs, and thought I was a slam dunk for another date.
- the one who freaked out over giving $.06 more than a 15% tip.
- the one who wanted to be exclusive at the salad course and told me that when I put a cherry tomato in my mouth. I almost spit it across the room.
- the one who tucked his sweatshirt into his jeans.

But the most bizarre encounter occurred before I met the guy.

The way match.com worked (back in my day) is you would view someone's profile, if you liked him, you would email him through the site and initiate a conversation. He could either ignore you or communicate back. And vice-versa. I preferred to pick the men I thought were potentially a good match for me and initiate the conversation rather than replying to those who picked me. Not sure why, but I wanted to be the picker. It's empowering to be the picker.

One day I received a message from Scott. He looked handsome in his profile picture, had a decent career, was well versed and seemed like a normal man. We began an email dialogue which flowed nicely. We wrote back and forth about 15 times and he asked if he could call me. I told him I would call him the next day (using *69 so my number was blocked). When we spoke on the phone Saturday afternoon, he opened up a bit more about his past and family situation and divulged that he had shared custody of their four-year old son. He also was not divorced yet. (Ding ding ding ding. If a red flag made a sound, it would ding four times.) He asked me if I would come to his house for a cookout the next day, which was Sunday. His friends, family and son would all be there. I was hesitant to say yes but he kept pleading and pleading with me, so on a whim I gave in and said yes, I'll be there.

We hung up and instantly, the discerning voice in my head screamed, "Gayle, you told yourself you would not date a married man! You also wanted to get to know a man before meeting his kids!"

This was a standard I made for myself. I would not get involved with a married man. There was too much risk involved. What if he went back to her? What if he had no intention of divorcing and I would be the other woman? Nope, not gonna happen. I wanted to be in control of my own dating experiences and this went against the standard I held for myself. No one else is going to lower my own standards except for me, and I wasn't willing to do that.

After about five minutes, I stopped screaming at myself. I called him back and gently explained how I was not comfortable meeting him, his son and entire family on our first encounter. I felt good about being perfectly honest and true to myself. I anticipated his reaction and expected it to go something like this. "Oh, I'm disappointed, but I understand. Would you like to meet for coffee or a bite to eat some other time? Just the two of us?"

Yeah, no, he didn't say that. Why would I expect a normal response? It's me we're talking about here. Here is his response:

"Oh Gayle! I told my entire family you were coming! You need to come! Do you know how many women have contacted *me* on match? Hundreds! And I picked you out of so many because you have all the qualities I want in a woman! By you not coming tomorrow, I feel like I'm in little league and the bases are loaded, two outs in the ninth inning and the coach tells me to go up to bat. I am so excited to be given this opportunity! Yeah me! Then he tells me to sit back down! That's how I feel here Gayle! I'm down and out in the ninth!

"Do you understand that I made a chart with all qualities I want in a woman and you are the **only one** with all gold stars? You have all gold stars Gayle and you won't come over and meet me? I don't know how I can go on. I really don't. I finally found the right person for me and you do this to me!! I am so down, how can I go on without meeting you!"

After what seemed like an eternity, I finally calmed him down by literally telling him everything that was wrong with me....and making some bizarre crap up so that he would peel all those gold stars off his chart.

See? I should have been the picker.

That literally was the end of match.com for me. I hope he found peace.

Geesh!

DO I STAY OR DO I GO GO?

There may come a time in your relationship when you say to yourself, "I don't know if this feels right, should I break up or wait it out?"

Honestly, that 'iffy' period is not fun. The uncertainty of whether you are growing together, feeling angst when you constantly fight over ridiculous stuff, questioning the level of effort he puts into the relationship, and the nagging in your head that something is way off. "Is this worth it?" "We are bickering an awful lot lately." "She seems aloof." "He's been going out with his friends more often than usual." "I just don't know how I feel now." "All the butterflies in my stomach have flown away."

As you develop closer as a couple, the make-a-great-impression phase fades. You become comfortable completely being yourself. You are past the woo because they are already wooed. The real person comes out. Sometimes it's minor stuff like, "Woah, I didn't realize she looked like *that* under her makeup!" "Could he just put the cap on the toothpaste once! Just once!!"

Then comes the next level of challenges. "She spends so much time partying with her friends and is out until all hours of the night." "He spent our savings betting on the Kentucky Derby and lost!"

So how do we decide when to remain in a relationship and when to leave? When you're thinking about calling it quits, your initial question might be, "Do I *really* want to break up? We were so happy once. I'm sure I can get that feeling back. Hang in there, things can change. After a heartfelt conversation about it, things might improve, but that improvement lasts 10 seconds and the same issues pop up again just like Whack-a-Mole. And then back to square one.

"I don't want to have to start over again. Dating ugh. I'll just stick it out. But the longer I stick, the unhappier I am."

I feel there is a time to give a relationship a chance, a time to detach if a break is needed to figure out what we really want, and then there is a time when we must make a decision to leave.

Here's a foolproof way to figure out when it's time to hang in or when to leave. This worked like a charm for me because it really put things into perspective and taught me how to make the right choice based on self-care and self-love.

If you are struggling with a decision, the most effective way to find your answer is to imagine your dilemma is happening to the person you love with all your heart. Could be your son, your mother, your pet Snoopy. Whoever, it is doesn't matter, just make sure you love this person unconditionally and you want what's best for her.

Pretend she is sitting across from you and sharing your exact situation just as you are experiencing it. From the perspective of loving her the way you do, tell her honestly what you feel about the situation and what you think she should do. From the point of view that you want the best for her, what would you tell her? Should she stay or should she go? If she gives you all the excuses you have given yourself, look at those excuses and be real with what exactly is going on. If she justifies bad behavior saying everyone will treat her badly, tell her there is a loving person out there waiting for her. Give her reasons why she needs to take care of herself. Everything will be okay.

This is a powerful exercise to do when you are having a tough time making up your mind. So many blocks and fears could be preventing you from making a rational decision. When you give advice to a loved one, in an objective manner, the process looks different. Because you love her unconditionally, you want what is best for her.

There is a time to stick it out, a time to wait and a time to leave. Confidently, you can choose whether *you* want to stay or go-go.

DATING DON'T, PLEASE!

For the most part, dating was not pleasant. I didn't fancy the pit in my stomach before I left the house. I didn't look forward to the awkward small talk. I felt uncomfortable with the instant knowing that this pairing was not going to work out and I had to go through the next hour feeling he wasn't interested and I would never see him again. Or vice versa. That happened to me with potato-drooler guy. As I witnessed the sour cream and chive froth formed on the side of his mouth and then drip down his chin, I sighed and waited the excruciatingly long 17 minutes for the date to end.

A couple of times though, I did look forward to a date. One man who lived in the next town was high on my potential mate scale. He had a child my daughter's age and appeared to be a normal, friendly, solid man. He had a job (there's a plus). We corresponded quite a bit by email. I asked him if he ever purchased any lick-em gold stars. He replied "No". He was good looking in his profile picture, well-groomed and showered regularly. No red flags! We talked and laughed on the phone several times and planned to meet later in the week.

There was above average potential with this guy. He emailed me the morning of our date and said he would meet me at 6 pm in the bar area of a local pub. I did not have a pit in my stomach that night. I left my house with a skip in my step and was looking forward to seeing where this would take us. At this point I was a dating pro, having been on 50 gabillion blind dates. I had the game down pat.

I walked into the bar area a few minutes early. I sat down, a little uncomfortable being alone, and scoped out the bar area. Although there were several single men slouched over, none of them matched his description. I ordered a strong girlie drink and waited. Every time someone walked through the door I glanced up, nope not him. Nope not him. After taking another sip, I looked down at my empty martini glass and over to my watch. 15 minutes late. Now, here's a thought-provoking dilemma. How long do you give a blind date to show up? Is it like the teacher ten-minute rule? When the professor does not show after ten minutes, it's customary for the students to bolt.

Honestly, I began to worry thinking that something bad must have happened. He confirmed that morning and said he was excited to meet me. Texting did not exist back then in the olden days and I did not have his number on my phone. What's a girl to do? I decided to go outside, sit on a bench and call a friend. She'll know what to do. After a 36-minute wait, I decided to go home. No date. I was pissed. I was concerned. Hope nothing happened. Well, something better had happened for him not to show up.

Note: If this had occurred on one of my first dates I would have thought, on no, it was me, my nose was too big, or I wasn't beautiful enough. Nope, not this time. I was so upset! Who tells a single woman to meet him at a place if he intends to stand her up? Ok, Gayle, don't jump too far ahead. Maybe there is an email at home.

Drove home, no email. No message. Now I'm angry. A gentleman or person with a pulse would never put a single woman in a situation where she sat alone in a bar. A breathing person would contact me and say: "I thought about it and I don't want to have a drink with you. I'm not into it and I'm going to stand you up." "I don't want you to sit by yourself in a bar at night." "I don't like you." "You stink." Any of these excuses would have been more appropriate than leaving me there thinking a piano fell out of the sky and onto his head.

A few months later, I started dating my future husband John. I didn't know he would be my husband at the time, but he showed up when he said he would show up and now he's my boyfriend. Big points.

On a random afternoon, I was checking out at the grocery store. Behind me was a man and his adorable daughter. He called her name and the hair stood up on my neck! I glanced over my shoulder and it was stood-me-up-guy! I was speechless. Same profile face, same rare daughter's name. Instantly, rage built up in me and I felt like giving him a piece of my mind, but had enough self-control to refrain, pay for my groceries and walk away with dignity (even though I wanted to throw my red-stickered watermelon at him). As I placed the last bag in my trunk, they walked by me to his car. Sitting in my car, I shifted in drive and slowly drove over him…I mean drove over **to** him. Pulling up by his side, I rolled down my window.

Gayle, are you seriously going to confront him? Yup, sure am. He helped his daughter in the backseat and shut her door.

I called out his name. "Kevin?"

Yes? He turned around and looked at me.

"Hi there, a few months ago we were supposed to meet at Friday's on a blind date and you never showed up. That was not cool. I wish you would have told me you changed your mind so I would not have had to sit in that bar alone. I would have understood. Please never do that to another woman. If you don't want to meet her, just have the balls to let her know so she is not placed in an uncomfortable and potentially unsafe situation. Have a nice afternoon. Goodbye." I was calm and articulate. I did not give him a second to speak.

As I began to drive away, he stood there with his mouth hanging open. I know this because I analyzed his every move in my rear-view mirror. I grew a pair that day and am proud that I used my voice! Hopefully this exchange helped him understand why he should never do that again. Not cool.

SINGLE PARENTING STRESS RELIEVERS

Dealing with life as a single parent is demanding and often pull-your-hair-out frustrating. When you have two parents living under the same roof with kids it can be stressful. Take away one parent and you are doing double the work, so the chaos increases twofold. I felt it bigtime. Juggling a million chores, rides, school projects, cleaning, soccer practice, self-care. I managed to get through by tweaking and adjusting situations along the way. Here are several tips that helped me maintain a sense of sanity.

Involve other parents:

When Becca was in elementary school, all the kids in the neighborhood and at least one of their parents stood in the rain, snow, sleet and windstorms at the bus stop at the end of our street. There were 5 parents in pajama pants and no makeup. I was in the middle of lean training at work and decided to put a kaizen into action. I asked if we could assign one parent to one day of the week to stand with the kids. If I left for work earlier, it would help me get home earlier, which would relieve a lot of stress. This was a win-win for all! We all exchanged numbers and assigned ourselves a day. If a child would not be at the bus stop that day, we would call the parent on duty to let them know.

Anyone with kids in sports knows that practices and games are just about every night and weekend. It is cumbersome to drive back and forth to every single practice, so why not ask another soccer parent who lives nearby to share rides? I would take their child home on Mondays and Wednesdays and they would take my daughter home on Tuesdays and Thursdays. Worked like a charm.

Schedule weekly play dates with your friend and your child's friend. On Mondays, my friend Cindy and I would take turns going to each other's homes for dinner. She prepared filet mignon wrapped in bacon with

Gorgonzola and homemade mashed potatoes and arugula salad. I told her to go to the freezer and pick out a Lean Cuisine. Becca and Cindy's children would play for hours in my toy room or Cindy's basement while we sat around enjoying mommy friend time.

Develop a support group:

Working full time required me to be in the office past 4 pm. Becca was home from school by 2:45 pm. There's the dilemma. I had to figure out how to handle that 2 hours. I posted a babysitter ad at our town library and high school. Wonderful young women came to the house one by one and after I interviewed them, I trusted my gut. I hired a caring young woman *and* a backup (which I thought was genius on my part!). Kara, Candace, Katie, Vicki, and Vanessa were instrumental in raising my little girl. They enhanced her life in remarkable ways. They were mature and reliable and helped relieve my stress on so many levels. They are lifelong influences in Becca's life.

Ask parents and grandparents and friends for babysitting help. My friend Melon used to babysit for Becca when I had a weekly meeting. Irene and Lisa babysat for her once when I had a bridal shower. I came home and my precious single friends were zonked out on the couch and Becca was bouncing up and down wide awake in her crib. When my college roommate Jan had twins, four of us went over to care for the twins for one night. She had two older children ages 3 and 6. Melon and I had the adorable (fussy) twin with the nail polish and Lisa and Irene were caring for the other baby who, of course, was quiet as a mouse. After all were fed and clean with fresh diapers, we took a cat nap together on the pull-out couch – only enough room for the 4 of us to spoon. We finally got to sleep around 5 am. A few minutes later I felt a tap on my shoulder. "I'm hungry." It was her 6-year-old. Yes, it takes a village. That was the last time this village babysat.

Don't be afraid to ask for help. Doing everything on your own is overwhelming and can result in major anxiety. Having grandparents,

145

friends, neighbors, or a trusted adult to rely on will provide a sigh of relief.

Make sure rules are reasonable and clear:

Oh, this caused me so much stress! Because I felt guilty over the divorce, I did not have the courage to follow through with some punishments. As a result, Becca could manipulate me to cave. That caused me stress. Eventually, I made a list and put it up on the refrigerator. I had a serious talk with her and explained the new rules. If she did this, then this is the consequence. I made them reasonable and followed through. It was a hard transition at first (which made me more stressed) but over time, she knew that I would follow through and life became so much easier.

I would also give her chores to do around the house. She was a member of the family and was responsible for her stuff. Why should I do everything? I was clear about her weekly chores: empty the dishwasher, do your own laundry, clean your room. Of course, they were age appropriate. Teaching her responsibility helped her become a strong, independent, hard-working adult.

Clear the clutter:

Yep, we all know that toy rooms become disaster rooms after holidays or birthday parties. She had so many toys. Half of them were not touched in months. I decided, after getting my toes stuck in her Barbie airplane for the last time, that enough was enough. From then on, once a new gift came into the house, she would select an old toy to donate. Over time, she became excited to help other less fortunate children. Sometimes she struggled to part with a stuffed animal, but she embraced this custom and I believe it taught her about giving and not being so attached to material things. Plus, I now had room to walk in her toy room without ripping off a toe!

Clothes are also a source of frustration. Kids grow out of things so quickly and it's easy for closets to become stuffed and busting out of the seams. Every few months or so I would go through her closet and donate her clothes. Sounds so simple but this is something that can get away from us and if we wait too long, it is a daunting process. Break the process into chunks. Go through socks one day, then onesies, then jammies. Whatever works. Becca was my big helper and would put all the clothes we were giving away into the laundry basket – after she dumped all the clothes and put the laundry basket on top of her head.

Find someone you can swap clothes with. If you know a younger child who would fit into your child's outgrown clothes, give them to her. Maybe you can swap with her older child or barter a babysitting night.

Hand-me-downs swaps are great for adults also. Ask a bunch of friends over and have a pot luck dinner and clothes swap night. Then donate all the leftover clothing. That's a trifecta win!
Someone told me once that a great way to get rid of anything in your house – clothes, clutter, shoes – is to put every single item in one of four piles.

Pile 1) Keep; Pile 2) Give away; Pile 3) Consign; Pile 4) Throw Out.

If you haven't worn an item of clothing in 6 months and it's in good shape, it goes in pile 2) or 3). I heard a wonderful idea about when it's time to get rid of clothes. Make sure all your hangers are facing one way. Once you wear a piece of clothing, turn the hanger around. After 6 months, review all the clothes you have not worn and make a hard decision whether you really want to keep it or not. If the hanger has not been moved in a year, it's time to get rid of it.

Make time for belly laughs:

So often we find ourselves frustrated, grumpy and crabby because we are over our heads with responsibilities and chores. If all we do is nag at the kids to do this, do that, don't do this, don't do that, we lose the opportunity to have memorable times. It's critical to occasionally let loose and spontaneously plan fun activities. Forget about the laundry or crud on the counters and pull out a board game or Twister and have some laughs. Have a random build-your-own-sundae night, plan a sleepover with a scavenger hunt, have the kids do impressions. A belly laugh will release stress and take frustration levels down several notches. And don't be surprised if the behavior of your wee munchkins improves. New motto. "Be goofy on purpose."

Practice Self Care:

Take a break. Get your nails done. Press the reset button and giggle at cartoons with the kids. Ask a friend to babysit while you go for a long walk. Self-care is so important for a single parent and it is also crucial for your children to see that you need a break. If you try to be superwoman and that is all your daughter sees, chances are she will develop the same habits. Kids have keen perceptions and they pick up on everything their parents do. It is healthy to show them that mommy or daddy need a time out to recharge their batteries.

These ideas have win-win results. There is no better way!

Part 3

MERGING THE FAMILIES

I AM WHO I AM WHO I AM

While on a dinner date, you won't see me eating a nibble of lettuce and a string bean. Bring on the meatball sub and the chocolate lava cake! If I have a cowlick gone astray, I will not cancel the date, I'll spread on the mousse, put my best cowlick forward and head out the door. I will not do a three-week colon cleanse before my blind date and pretend that my stomach is flatter than it is.

I know for a fact I'll be rejected time and again, **_but_** the one who is interested in me will want the real me, not some fake version of me.

I spent a tremendous amount of time and energy restoring my broken self to be comfortable in my own skin and accept by entire being. I was not going to dumb it down, expose my bazookas or pretend I'm someone I'm not to impress a guy I don't know from a hole in the wall.

Don't get me wrong, I'll shower, suck on a tic-tac and put my best wide feet forward, but I will not exaggerate or give the illusion I am someone I am not. I will express my true feelings and if he doesn't agree, I will not take it personally nor will I stray from what I truly believe.

Thing is, I now own who I am. I don't have to make excuses for who I am anymore. I don't have to apologize for not being perfect. I don't have to take on other people's issues and accept behaviors that are unacceptable. I don't have to be desperate for attention and affection. I don't have to feel that I am damaged goods.

I can trust my instincts. I can go out with a new man, be my bubbly, goofy self and walk away feeling confident and self-assured – no matter what he thought of me. I can be secure with myself in and out of a relationship. The man I end up with will adore me for me, and not for the me that hooked him in by false advertising.

150

It becomes dangerous territory when you transform your whole being to fit into someone else's life. When you say what you think he wants to hear, do the things you don't want to do just to please him, and stuff your wants and desires way down deep, you are not being true to your authentic self. This is the recipe for losing yourself.

Eventually the true essence of who we are seeps out. Might as well show the true colors right away. Might save you and your date a whole lot of time and drama.

When I am completely myself on a date, I might be turned down and rejected or I might be adored and pursued. It might be refreshing to the person sitting opposite me to be with someone who is the real deal. Who knows, he might become my Forever Boyfriend.

WHO WINS FOR BEING THE WORST DATER?

Umm, that would be John. Although if you asked him, he would say me.

Our love story began at the salad bar of our cafeteria. To this day John is adamant that we did not talk at the salad bar. He claims we spoke at the grill. (psst: It really was at the salad bar.)

John and I were acquaintances for years before we started dating. We both worked for the same company and brought our children to the same daycare. When we first met, each of us were married. I thought he and his wife were a nice couple. We usually sat near each other during magic shows and pancake breakfasts. John and his wife were laid off from our company and it was years later when I randomly saw him again at jury duty. We exchanged pleasantries and I was called to serve and he was let off the hook.

A few years later, I bumped into John in our work cafeteria. He was wearing a blue suit and tie and looked handsome. He was on an interview and having lunch with his soon-to-be boss.

I tapped him on the shoulder and said, "Hi! You're back?"

After a bit of small talk, we shared that we were both split from our spouses. "Good luck John! Hope you get the job!" I smiled a great big white-stripped toothy smile and off he went to eat his salad.

I felt a sparkle. I always liked him. He was kindhearted and seemed like a loving father. I flashed back to an argument my ex and I were having several years prior. He and I were in the car bickering before we picked up Becca from daycare. John was picking up his kids at the same time. As John walked in front of our car and waived, I distinctly remember thinking how cute he was. Boyish charm.

Check.

A few months after he was hired, I asked him to be on a March of Dimes walk event committee that I was chairing. I did not know much about him personally but thought this was a perfect way to get to know him better. He reluctantly accepted after I went heavy on the charm.

At one point I invited him to a singles party one of my cruise girl pals was throwing. I made sure he knew I was inviting other single male friends. I didn't want him to think he was the only one I invited. I guess it was a bit of a mixed message but I didn't want him to know I liked him until I knew he liked me. Yes, I was acting like a 12-year old. He ended up skipping the party because he coughed. I was quite disappointed. He showed up at my desk Monday morning explaining what happens during his coughing fits. Bla, bla bla bla.

I curtly replied, "You missed a fun time," and turned my back on him and pretended to type some urgent email on my computer. I was not going to waste my time with this guy. If he wanted to be with me, he would have stopped coughing and come to the party. Surprisingly though, before he left my cubicle, he asked if I wanted to go with him to Six Flags the following Saturday…without the kids.

After spending an hour picking out an appropriate I'm-not-sure-if-this-is-a-date outfit, I settled on a dark heavy knit sweater and cute shorts. I neglected to check the weather forecast for the day and it was blisteringly hot and humid. While standing in line waiting to get on the Superman roller coaster, I knew I was in trouble when I felt drips of sweat flow down my back. I could tell my face was beet red and mascara was smudged under my eyes. We went on the rolling rapids to cool off and of course, the waterfall pounded directly on me. I was completely drenched with slimy, chilly water, and boy did it feel refreshing!

I bought a t-shirt to change into and as I checked myself in the mirror, I was totally convinced this would be our one and only outing together. And the icing on the cake? The wetness from my bra seeped through my light gray t-shirt making two huge dark gray boob spots. Oh my God! I belonged in a horror movie! When he dropped me off at home, I basically said, "I had fun!" and ran out of the car.

Unbelievably, he called and asked me to go to lunch. We were still in the friend zone but getting more comfortable with each other. We played a work golf tournament, went to lunch together, and flirted a lot, but still in the friend zone. I wasn't going to make the first move, and apparently, neither was he. Our platonic lunch dates were set up that he paid, then I paid, until one lunch when I took care of the bill, he said okay, he would let me pay this one, as long as he paid for the next meal, but it had to be dinner. Which to me meant a weekend. Was he asking me on a date? Not sure. No clue. Whatever it meant, I had no problem eating.

He picked me up and we arrived at a trendy seafood restaurant about 30 minutes away. We had a few drinks and divulged more and more about ourselves. He suggested we go to a movie afterwards. It was very attractive that he printed off the movies and times beforehand and had it at his disposal in his glove box.

Check.

As we pulled up my driveway after the Six Flags debacle, I bolted in the house without asking him to come in. But after this great evening, I didn't run away, I invited him in. He said yes.

We watched something on TV and talked for a bit. We spent hours and hours together and he did not bug me. That was unusual because I had a habit of picking men apart and something they did always bugged me. John was somewhat shy, genuine and funny and we had no trouble communicating. Why didn't he make a move? I wasn't going to make a move– no way. I'm the gift.

154

As he was getting ready to go leave, we stood in the hallway and behold our suave conversation:

John: "So, are we dating?"

Gayle: "I don't know. Are we?"

John: "I don't know. Do you want to?"

Gayle: "I don't know, do you?"

John: "Sure. I wasn't sure because I tried to hold your hand in the movie theatre and you shooed me away."

Gayle: "That was you? I thought it was a bug."

After that painful exchange the night concluded with a couple of smooches, smiles and hugs. We both wiped our brows feeling grateful that the awkwardness was behind us and we could now move forward as a new adorable couple.

Check-mate!

IS THERE A MOSQUITO IN THE ROOM?

Quirky little habits of your new boyfriend or girlfriend are so precious….at first.

You were fixed up on a blind date. You connected on a cosmic level. You will never wash your lips again! You want to have babies with him! Every spare moment you have, you want to be with him. He's perfect for you! In every way. On every day.

A few weeks in, he accidentally lets out a high-pitched squeaker at a fancy dinner party. He grins, turns to you and points to the guy behind him. You chuckle underneath your breath thinking that he is so funny! On your 8th date as you're hanging out at his apartment, you open a closet door and 6 months of laundry bust out onto the floor. You feel badly that he doesn't know how to work the washing machine. Poor guy!

For two hours, she engages you in conversation about the latest office gossip and in detail describes every feeling she has about the situation. You think it's great that she confides in you. You both are watching an action movie that you couldn't wait to watch. She asks you questions during the whole movie. Oh, she values my opinion!

A few months later, he intentionally toots in front of your parents. You gasp and say he's disgusting! He tosses another dirty dish in the sink, you murmur under your breath, can you wash **one** dish?

She talks non-stop during movie night. He rolls his eyes and turns up the volume. She takes forever to get ready and he sits in the car trying not to blow his stack. She comes home and talks about her feelings for two hours, then takes a bath and still rambles on about the same story! His eyes glaze over.

I swear we go into another dimension when we are first dating someone. The things that normally would drive us crazy seem to be adorable. Like a puppy. Everything a puppy does is cute. Look how precious he is eating my shoe! Chewing through the front door is good for his teeth! Oh, he messed on the rug, it's okay, you're a good boy!

Early on, we get to know each other and find out quirky things about each other. We are connecting on a higher level and it feels euphoric. Like walking on a cloud. We just want to be with this person no matter what. Nothing fazes us, nothing upsets us, it's all bliss.

Men tend to take less time exposing their quirks. Women, sometimes, need a more time to let their guard down. Months or even years into a relationship, we may ask him to leave the house for an hour or two when we need to use the bathroom. Believe it or not, this is a common thing.

Things seem to be set on temporary hold when you begin dating someone special. Then, at some point reality sets in. You must work a full day. The huge pile of clothes on your floor is standing up by itself screaming for a soap pod. Your floor is now covered in a layer of grit. Your bills have red overdue stamps on them. Your pets don't recognize you. All these things must now be tended to. You can no longer afford to buy new underclothes when you run out. It's time to return to normalcy.

Five weeks after John and I started dating, we booked and paid for a cruise that would set sail seven months into the future. $2,000 per person. Yep, five weeks in. We both said we had a back-up plan if we happened to break up, but we really didn't. I'm sure one of my friends would have jumped at the chance to go had we broken up, but at the time I thought there was no way we would ever break up. Geesh, we would never even have an argument! He's perfect!

And you discover more pesky things that can drive you crazy about your partner once you live together. Things we thought were once precious, are not so precious anymore. You must get used to his idiosyncrasies and he must get used to yours. I'm talking about the things that are not deal breakers but the things that can get under your skin. Like ants in your pants.

I like to keep the house at 60 degrees. This was something that John has learned to embrace, or so I say, because he had no choice in the matter. If he went through menopause, he could pick the temperature, but fortunately for him... I also like to keep the bedroom a little below 60 – sometimes at 57 or 58 degrees. One time in the winter I accidentally turned the thermostat down to 41 degrees. When we walked into the room we could see our breath. It was shocking when we first jumped into bed because the sheets were frozen, but after a few minutes under the covers, it became cozy and warm. John tells his friends he sleeps in a meat locker. His solution is to wear layers. It works!

When first married to my ex, I did his laundry and he had a bunch of striped rugby shirts. Every time I did the wash, the dark red stripe would seep into the white stripe and the white would come out with pink streaks. I tried to wash them so many times, even hand wash them, and that stupid white streak always smeared. After watching him get upset that I ruined his latest birthday present, I started to place his defective shirts in the garbage. I must have thrown out 15 shirts. I convinced myself that he wouldn't look for them in the garbage can! Until one day when he came home holding a white and pink blotted striped shirt and said, "Gayle, is there something you want to tell me?" I could have been a tiny gnat in the room that day.

John tends to sneeze 40 times in a row when he gets into a fit. It's exhausting to say, "Bless You" 40 times, so after the 10th time I'll yell, "Shut the hell up!" with a huge smile on my face. See, I found a way to make it work.

Just the other day I was working at a new job and John had to take our kitty to the vet. This was her first visit so he had to fill out her information. She is basically gray with a bit of orange tossed in. I receive his first text. "What color is she?" Oh, my precious little mosquito!

We gradually come to know what to expect and figure out ways make it work. It is critical that after the euphoric stage starts to pass into reality, we continue to press on. If we are with the right person, those mosquitoes in the room won't matter.

THE FIRST FEW ENCOUNTERS

After several months of dating, John and I decided it was time to introduce the kids to one another. Becca had met John once in my work cafeteria and when I told her I was dating him she said, "You mean that cute guy I met at lunch?" I nodded and smiled. She had great taste!

Nick, Becca and Dan were 6,7 and 8 respectively when we all met for the first time. We went to an Armory Museum and out for a treat. The kids were checking each other out and didn't utter a word except for YES! when asked if they wanted ice cream. It was okay for a first meeting but there was not a lot of interaction.

At our next meeting we decided to kick it up a notch and go to an interactive activity. We went to a corn maze where we would have to find clues relating to the park pirate theme. We figured the kids would engage with one another. The maze was huge. There were 6 bridges throughout the maze and at each bridge we would receive a stamp and candy, and once completed the kids would receive a coin. It sounded like the perfect day for family fun. It was difficult to maneuver around the 8-foot corn husks and it was tough to find the first bridge. We had to walk single file and Nick was in the lead for the first hour or so. We still couldn't find a bridge so I decided to lead the troops. Immediately we passed a freeze pop wrapper lying on the ground. A few minutes later we passed the same freeze pop wrapper. The kids were like, "We just saw that wrapper!" I assured them I knew where I was going! After we walked past the freeze pop wrapper for the 5th time, Nick said to John, "Dad, do we have to listen to that lady anymore?" We had an amazing day and the bonding began!

The boys would stay with us every other weekend and John would take them to dinner a few times during the week. We managed to get the kids on the same weekend, so John and I would have a weekend with the kids and a weekend without.

It was important to have together time with everyone. We learned about geocaching, a free and adventurous outdoor activity where you use GPS coordinates to find hidden treasures. We would go to state parks to hide and seek containers. The containers are waterproof and contain a logbook, a pencil and many have little treats like a ball, yoyo, deck of cards. It was so much fun going through the woods and finding our way via coordinates. The kids sometimes had to climb a tree to find the container, one time it was at the end of a branch that fell over across a pond. Quite a challenge for the little tree monkeys! We'd bring backpacks with snacks and would go out for hours. Didn't cost a penny, except for the granola bars and juice boxes.

Over time, we ventured out and went to a lot of cool places. I loved going to plays and we would attend local theatre for a bit of culture. We sat in the front row at the Christmas Carol and one of the actors was talking right in front of us and a piece of spittle landed on Dan's cheek. We never sat in the front row again. We would go to museums, fairs, movies, vacations, and

Activities are so critical when introducing and merging families. It's a wonderful way to get to know one another and have some fun.

OUR WEDDING

John popped the question to me while we were on a horse and buggy ride in Newport RI. It was a spectacular day, not a cloud in the sky. I was commenting on the perfect day and he stared into my eyeballs and said, "Want to make it more perfect?" He pulled out a ring and I screamed YES! It was very romantic!

John and I decided to have the actual wedding ceremony on our own and then have a intimate dinner with close family and friends afterward. Our destination wedding took place in Lake Tahoe after a 5 day getaway at the exquisite Ahwahnee Hotel in Yosemite National Park. It was like 4 million dollars a night but we didn't care, we were getting married! We saw breathtaking views, gigantic trees and drove on a windy road with a 3,000-foot drop. John drove with white knuckles all the way – he wouldn't even peek at the spectacular view!

The morning before we were about to leave for Lake Tahoe, we were lying in bed talking about the wedding. Out of nowhere, these gremlin-like thoughts popped into my head. "Oh no, what if *this* marriage doesn't work out? What's worse than one divorce? Two divorces? I can't go through with this! I'm scared to death. I can't go through *another* divorce!" John didn't have a clue what was going on in my mind, but he knew something was up when I started gagging. He asked, "What's wrong honey?" I told him I didn't want to get divorced!!! I got up and went to the bathroom, threw up and sat on the side of the tub until I composed myself. Deep breath in, deep breath out. About 1000 times.

I finally left the bathroom and hopped back into bed. Sorry, I just had to barf for a minute. John was so comforting. He held me and reassured me that we would be okay and how much he valued and appreciated me. He couldn't predict the future but knew we were solid and in love and he repeatedly told me how happy he was. He was talking from his heart and
162

gently consoled me. That meant the world to me.

Now I was ready to hold his hand and take a second plunge in the marriage pool.

We headed off to our magnificent wedding destination in southern Lake Tahoe. The owner of our B&B was also a minister and a boat captain. He suggested we get married on his boat right on the lake. Simple, charming, romantic, just the two of us. I wore an elegant, champagne, twinkly gown and John brought his best suit. Stop and Shop supplied my roses and we headed down to the dock.

Our B&B owner/ boat captain / minister / preparer of our breakfast was waiting for us while maneuvering his Gilligan's Island boat close to the dock. He navigated around the lake and gave us a lovely tour. He shared celebrity stories as we passed by an Inn where Frank Sinatra and Sammy Davis Jr and the rest of the brat pack frequently stayed. In order to officiate the actual wedding ceremony, we had to drift from Nevada to California to the proper place where he officially could marry us. It was such a peaceful, quaint ceremony. We both said, "I Do!!" sealed it with a kiss and thought, "Now what?" So, we called the kids!

We are now a blended family! We polished off a bottle of champagne and headed back to shore. The photographer was waiting for us on the beach at the B&B. As we walked toward the beach area as Mr. and Mrs., I saw a nice couple sitting on the stairs near our cottage. I glanced over to them, smiled, turned away. Then did a double take. It was Irene and Mike, our friends from home! What a surprise! Their initial plan was to swim up to the boat during our vows, but instead they patiently waited for us to come back to the cottage. Apparently, they did some magician-like moves so we wouldn't run into them.

We had a lovely few days together. We went to the set of the Bonanza television show. The men found it fascinating, Irene and I were like – eh. Hoss and Little Joe didn't mean much (*anything*) to us. We had a delicious dinner and said goodbye to our ultra-cool friends as we continued on with our honeymoon.

Although our actual ceremony was just the two of us, we had the dinner celebration to look forward to back at home. We rented a charming restaurant and invited 50 of our closest friends and family. The venue was warm and cozy, any more than 50 guests would have been too crowded. The owner said there would be five tables of ten. Several days prior to the dinner, I dropped off the seating chart and table setting cards.

On Saturday October 10th, we dressed the kids up fancy for the wedding dinner. I bought Nick and Dan boutonnieres and Becca a floral wrist corsage. Becca and I went to my hairdresser Kelli so she could bouffant our hair for the special day. The kids looked so cute! I remember running around like a madwoman finalizing the details that day. In total all I had to eat was one munchkin from Dunkin Donuts. I had no time to eat anything else.

When we arrived at the restaurant about a half-hour prior to the guests' arrival, the owner told me they had to rearrange the room and instead of 5 tables of 10, there would be 4 tables of 12. In a normal situation this shouldn't have been a big deal, but there were some who were not comfortable sitting near each other. I was irritated that the owner didn't tell me beforehand rather than springing it on me a few minutes before everyone arrived.

I had to really think about how to adjust the seating chart. I asked a waitress to pour me a Cosmopolitan because I was stressing out. People started showing up and I was not finished yet. Luckily there was a cocktail hour to give me a time buffer to figure things out. I was handed a few more cosmos by the waitstaff by the time I finished.

Three cosmos and one munchkin. It was 6 pm and that's all I put in my body that day. Ten minutes later I walked up to John and said something like "I took care of it," which came out like "EEEEY CHUKARE

OZNIT."

He looked at me a bit shocked and asked, "What the hell happened to you? Are you drunk?"

"Yup! And I looooooove you!" I leaned over and kissed him inside his ear.

Then I turned to the waiter, "I love you too!" I twirled around, kissed the waitress on the lips, and said, "I love yooooooooooou!" Spreading the love to all, whether I knew them or not.

The kids were enjoying themselves too, although not as much as me. I found out later that Becca, Dan and their cousin Kelly were throwing carrots and broccoli off the deck and into the pool below. Nick had spent the entire evening attached to John, like an appendage. He did not leave his side. Nick at one point said to John, "Gee, Gayle's pretty drunk."

This was the first time I was annihilated in front of John or the kids and many of our 50 guests. Although some had already seen me in that rare form - alias Jody Cote – this was a first for John. Luckily, I'm a happy drunk and he didn't ask for an annulment the next morning.

I cherished all who celebrated with us.

I just wish I could have remembered it.

DATE NIGHTS

When you date someone with kids and you have kids, the process of everyone getting to know the new family members takes time. Your relationship with your boyfriend and your own children is already established, but dynamics change even within those relationships. I decided it was important to schedule specific date nights to develop closer bonds with each family member.

<u>John and Gayle</u>

I wanted to spend a significant amount of time with just the two of us. I did not want to introduce the kids until John and I were solid and committed. I also didn't want to cut meat while trying to find out about John's childhood and what kind of pizza he liked. John and I had our kids on the same weekends, so we would spend every other weekend dating and having fun.

<u>Gayle and Becca</u>

It was important for me to continue having Papa Gino's night or go to our special park. Becca and I were alone for 5 years and I wanted to ease the transition of John and the boys entering her life. After she met John, she would get insecure sometimes and I thought it was important that I spend quality time with her alone. We did this once a week or so. This date solidified in her mind that she was still my priority.

<u>John and Nick and Dan</u>

Same thing for John. They would go to the movies or dinner and do boy stuff. It was as important for the boys to feel secure with John dating as well, although they were less drama than Becca.

Nick, Becca and Dan

Maybe it was not a typical 'date' night, but the three kids needed to spend time together. At first, they were shy around each other but quickly grew into a real sibling relationship. We finished the basement so they could have their own space to watch TV and play games.

John, Gayle, Nick, Becca and Dan

All five of us. Doing special things with the kids. Movies, mazes, geo caching, hikes, fishing, camping. So many memories!

We would have movie night, shut all the lights, put on some candles, pop a bunch of popcorn and watch a scary or stupid movie in the living room. No phones allowed, just all of us hanging out.

We also decided that we should also have one on one time with the kids on their birthdays. I would take Nick and Dan out a restaurant of their choice and give them $50 to go shopping with afterwards.

Gayle and Nick; Gayle and Dan

These nights are so special. It is when the kids really opened up or said nothing at all. You know boys – Yup, Nope. I learned to ask open questions so they could not answer Yup or Nope so we had to have a dialogue. Once they got comfortable with me, they didn't stop talking. Best to talk to the kids about school, their interests, friends, favorite subjects or hobbies, sports. Make it about them and build rapport.

I took Dan shopping for his 8th birthday so he could pick out a gift for himself. We walked by the men's section and he stopped dead in his tracks. He pointed to the packaged picture of the well-endowed male model in his white briefs and said, "That's just disturbing."

Still cracks me up.

167

John and Becca

Becca asked John to take her to Build a Bear on her first birthday date. She was 7 years old. Being the father of two boys who loved swords and policemen, John was in unfamiliar territory. He stood in line with other mothers as Becca sewed, washed, and fluff and puffed her bear. He said she did not stop talking from the second they left the house until he pulled in the driveway. He didn't even have to ask her leading questions, hell, he didn't have to ask her any questions. She volunteered it all and absolutely loved date nights.

The kids are in their twenties now and we still have date nights and look forward to them so much!!!

WHO SAYS YOU CAN'T HANG OUT WITH YOUR SPOUSE'S EX?

Years ago, I worked with a wonderful woman named Nancy. Nancy's husband, Jerry, had been married and divorced to another woman, Margaret. This was Nancy's first and only marriage. Nancy would tell me that she was going away for a night with Margaret. She took day trips and shopped with Margaret all the time. They got along brilliantly. My first thought as I listened to this was "How on earth can you be friends with your ex-husband's wife?" I was in my 20's and seeing how my mother and father couldn't even be in the same town together, never mind room, I could not comprehend this this concept. Not even a teeny-weeny bit. Nancy said, "Just because Margaret and Joe's marriage didn't work out, doesn't mean either one of them is a bad person. Margaret and I get along great and I enjoy her." Wow, this was a shocker to me, but I guess that's how some people roll.

Then I'd read in the tabloids how Demi and Bruce would co-parent and they got along wonderfully. They were amicable and not hostile and hateful toward each other.

Interesting. Guess there is another way.

When John and I started dating, we each knew each other's ex's. I liked her and John liked him. We all initially met when we our kids attended the same daycare center. We sat together at Santa's breakfast and puppett shows. We were friendly and cordial when we dropped the kids off. It was nice to feel how pleasant our interactions were.

That's not to say there weren't bumps here and there during the split, but we all had the kids in the forefront of our minds when it came to their parents. We refrained from any negativity and made sure the kids

169

respected their parents and observed our respect for them also.

The interaction with our exes basically centered around dropping off and picking up the kids and any school related activities. I had no problem saying hi to Becca's dad at a soccer game or sitting in the same section during a band concert when Becca honked her clarinet. John and his ex-wife had pleasant interactions which mostly revolved around the boys.

Since my ex and I attended the same college, we have a lot of mutual friends. I am more outgoing and continued to socialize with them. They would always ask how he is and one day I asked my ex and his girlfriend if they'd like to meet out. I shared pictures of all of us on Facebook and my friends are like, "Is that you and John and your ex and his girlfriend??" They laughed but at the same time thought it was cool that we were able to put our past behind us and enjoy a night with old friends.

Since then, we have gone on a few dinner dates together, the last being a cookout at Becca and her boyfriend's home. I know Becca is comfortable knowing that she can invite all of us to an event and not worry. Period. No worry, anxiety or tension. It's probably not my husband or ex's best scenario, but we all come together for the sake of our children. And it works.

Nick joined the Army when he was 18 and was abruptly deployed overseas. He was gone 9 months and we had very little contact with him. It had the potential to be a dangerous assignment. It was a tense time to say the least. When he came home on leave after his deployment we wanted to do something special for him. We asked him to think about it.

A few days later he said, "You know what I want to do? I want to go on a cruise with the whole family. Mom and Dad, Dan, Becca and you."

We all knew this would have made Nick very happy and after the sacrifice he just made, we all agreed to go. We booked a weeklong cruise to the Caribbean. We ate dinners together every night and all was pleasant and enjoyable. The highlight for me was, while during an excursion, watching tipsy Nick and his tipsy mom run through the knee-high ocean water to catch the 'punch man' before he ran out of drink of the day. I sat on the smaller boat and watched the two of them try to chase the guy with the red pitcher of happy juice.

As Nancy once told me, there doesn't have to be strife between the exes. There is a better way.

Not everyone is perfect, and you don't have to love your partner's ex, but it makes all the difference in the world when you can develop a cordial relationship with them. If you find things in common like gardening or the Patriots or a TV show, then you can build on that for the limited time that you spend together.

The children witness our interactions and it's critical to show them that the two people who brought them into this world can be civil and get along, for their sake.

I DON'T EVEN KNOW WHAT THAT MEANS

Going through a childhood living with an alcoholic mother had a major impact on my life. As a child, I never knew what to expect with my mother. On days when she was sober, she could be in a good mood and hysterically funny, yet other sober days she was critical and harsh. On days when she had been drinking, I knew to stay away. Make myself invisible. Hide in my room and pop in an 8 track tape; hang in the basement; or lick-kissed by my dog Mike in the backyard. If she locked herself in her bedroom for a long period of time, I would roam the house, but knew once her door opened, something would happen. And it usually wasn't good.

On any given day, I learned to think a few moves ahead so I could fly under the radar to avoid her verbal lashings. For all the years I lived with her, I lived in fear and walked on eggshells. I walked around with a constant pit in my stomach. I never knew what move would set her off. I would watch the Red Sox one day and all would be fine. The next day I would watch the Red Sox and all was not fine. Life was unpredictable, plain and simple.

That was my normal upbringing. Because I had been invited to a few birthday party sleepovers, I watched closely how my friends were treated. I realized that the uncertainty and anxiety I felt daily was not the norm. Yet, I didn't know how to exist any other way. Just like I never knew what a flat stomach felt like.

Fast forward to my late 30's when I met John. Dating him, marrying him, knowing him, trusting him, living with him, I learned there is another way to live.

He is even keeled. He has the same temperament at 9:03 am and at 2:40

pm. He is solid like a rock. I call him the flatliner. He loves me the same today, yesterday and (fingers crossed) tomorrow. He allows me to be who I am and does not judge me. We can have a disagreement without calling each other foul and hurtful names.

Being with him allowed me to be free.

And safe.

Many times when his is holding me at night, I will tell him how safe I feel. And that I'm so grateful to feel safe. And he makes me feel safe.

His honest reply. "Hon, I don't even know what that means."

With tearful eyes, I respond. "It means everything."

MONEY GROWS ON TREES, RIGHT KIDS?

Going from a family of two to a family of five is a momentous change. Lifestyle change and budget change. I went through a money transition when I divorced so I was used to cutting back but merging this family I felt differently. Because we were back to two incomes we thought it would be less strained. Things don't always happen as we imagine.

Every time I took Becca shopping she would ask me to buy practically everything in the store for her. We walked past board games, she wanted one; we walked past big plastic balls, she wanted those. I sprinted past the Barbie aisle, or avoided it altogether, because that would be my demise, but then she'd see stuffed animals and I was in trouble. When she was a toddler and old enough to understand simple reasoning, I told her that she could hold on to a stuffed animal while we were in the store but we had to return him to his 'home' when we left the store. It worked wonders until it didn't. Then I hired a babysitter and shopped alone.

When we went out with all three kids, we had to find events they would all enjoy. Going to a ball game was pricey for a family of five, but we thought a trip to NYC and a Yankees game would be awesome. The stadium is impressive. We happened to pick the hottest day on record over the last thousand years. We were in right field and the sun was beaming directly on us. We ordered five rounds of water during the game. $125.00! Plus, the kids might have been too young to appreciate the coolness of the electric city. We paid to get up to the top floor of the Empire State Building and 33 seconds after looking out over the gorgeous view, the kids asked what else we were going to do, because standing on top of the Empire State building was boring.

Next, because of the horribly dull view on top of one of the world's tallest structures, we took a walk over the Brooklyn Bridge and hopped on the Staten Island ferry. On the way to the island we passed the Statue of Liberty. Surely this would pique their interest. As we sailed by, tears welled up in my eyes. She was stunning. I had not seen her up close since I was a young girl. Dan, on the other hand, was fascinated with the dirty bubbles and foam that the ferry produced on the Hudson. The Statue of Liberty was right before our eyes, proud, strong, a symbol of freedom and Dan completely missed it because he was looking down at the filthy bubbles.

All in all, that NYC trip cost almost $3,000. Highlights were bottled water and brown suds.

When texting was introduced, we did not update our phone plan immediately, but told the kids not to use "the text". They could call whomever they wanted but were asked not to type to them. We didn't have a clue what it cost, but figured since the kids were pre-teens, we didn't have to worry about it.

The following month after we set the boundary for the kids not to text, our phone bill was $835.00. After I gained consciousness, I looked at the dates and something was not right. The dates where the text charges occurred was when the entire family was together driving to Niagara Falls. The two numbers on the bill who texted to and from each other were Nick and Becca's numbers. They happened to be sitting one row apart from each other in the minivan. Basically, instead of turning around and talking to each other, they texted one another during the whole drive from Massachusetts to Canada.

After John's heart rate and mad vein on his forehead returned to normal, we talked to the kids and told them under NO circumstances are they to text again. At all. Not even a little bit.

One month later, I had complete confidence the kids learned their lesson and never wanted to see John's popping veins again. $580.00 WTF!?!#!! These were the texts on the drive back from Canada to Massachusetts. I should have been pleased that it was less than the last bill, but somehow that thought didn't comfort me. I looked at the dates again and they did all this texting prior to our discussion with them. The dates after we told them NO were text free. Good, rotten kids.

I called the phone company and added the entire family to a text plan. It was $10 extra per month.

Since then we text for everything. I text John while we are in bed because the air conditioner is loud, and in my defense, we have a king-sized bed, so he's way over there. We will text each other while sitting next to each other watching a movie in the living room. Guess it's our new way of life.

On that same Niagara Falls trip, I left John in charge of the kids for about an hour while I did some shopping on my own. Big mistake. They went into the candy store. You know the store where individual pieces of candy are screaming for the kids to fill the big plastic bag as much as they possibly could? Three small kids in a candy store with free reign. What could possibly go wrong? $160.00 for penny candy. That's 16 million pennies, right?

We would go to the Jersey Shore with John's family every summer. Wonderful place, fun nights with his family. Kids had a blast playing in the pool and going to the boardwalk. The boardwalk was a kid's paradise, with 3 water parks, 3 separate piers with tons of rides and games and loads of fried food and fried Oreos! We had to purchase tickets to go on the rides, rather than paying a one-time fee for everything. That's the rub. Plus, the games are set up so that a kid had to play at least 50 games to win a plastic whistle. Do you see where I'm going with this?

After a few nights on the boardwalk and spending hundreds of dollars on blow pops and 2-inch stuffed animals, we had to come up with a different financial solution or we'd have to file for bankruptcy.

Since they were younger than 12, we couldn't put them to work at a traditional job, but we could have them do chores around the house, which they did. I also had to come up with a plan to make them responsible for their own spending money. John and I were done being an ATM machine. Once that vacation was over, we told the kids that they would have to bring their birthday or Christmas money on vacation. I was also going to save spare change during the year and I told them I would split it three ways so they can have some extra money. This idea resulted in $35 per kid. Not bad for a bunch of nickels.

The next year was drastically different. Instead of dishing out $3.00 per game now, there was a lot of pause whether they actually wanted to spend their own money to play. Dan was very frugal and smart, because he spent very little of his own money and had extra money when he came home. Becca blew threw her money on the first night.

Eventually it worked. Trial and error.

PARENTING STYLES

Becoming a married couple, living together after being single and adapting to your partners lifestyle is quite an adjustment. Throw in a couple of kids and the transition under one roof can be overwhelming.

This is my point of view. Take it or leave it, these suggestions I have learned and lived, and they have had a positive effect on the family.

It is imperative that the two adults have conversations about parenting and how they will parent moving forward. This discussion will be best if done *before* you merge. Get out some paper and go over different scenarios and discuss how you will handle if the situation comes up when the kids are living with you. This is obviously for children who are younger and not grown adults.

- How will we handle it if the kids fight with each other?
- What if one kid is being mean to the other kid?
- What if one of the kid's disrespects me?
- How do we handle if they don't listen to our household rules?
- What if they skip school?
- How do we handle holidays and gift giving?

Obviously, this list is just scratching the surface, so make up questions that you think might come up. When you are open with this kind of discussion, you have the choice to voice your opinion and how you would deal with it. If your partner and you differ, try to come up with a unified way to handle the situation so that it works for both of you.

John and I came up with rules when the kids were living with us. If they would fight over who got to use the computer, we would get out an egg timer and limit their time so each had a half hour. If they were willing to give up their time on the computer for more time on the Wii, so be it, they had to work it out among themselves. If they were fighting with each other and calling each other names, I had a hard rule that they had to say, "Be quiet, loving step-brother / step-sister," instead of "Shut Up!" They thought it was stupid at first, but I was adamant that there was to be no name calling or mean talk in our house.

There is a fine line when disciplining step children. Reality is that John and his ex-wife are Nick and Dan's parents.

So, what is my role as a step parent? I believe my role is to be an adult role model. To introduce them to different activities, make sure they are respectful, use their manners, expose them to different activities and adventures, to enforce rules of my home, to care for them when they are sick, to keep them safe, to build a solid relationship with them, to treat each child equally, to make them feel like they are part of the whole family unit, to correct them if they are wrong, to help with school projects, to teach responsibility, to be there when they need help, to teach them that they are expected to assist in household chores, to listen to their concerns, to make sure they treat all members of the family with consideration, and to set clear boundaries if they are out of line.

Once everyone knows what is expected and on the same page, boundaries are clear, and everyone settles into a routine. Problems arise when the bio parent and step parent cannot agree on how to handle certain situations. The parenting styles are not in sync and each parent is dealing with his/her own kids in a manner not consistent with the other parent. When it is extreme, this lack of balance has been the demise of some marriages. They could not figure out a way to make it work. That's why it is beneficial to discuss rules before you meld the two families together.

Step back, step parent.

If there is a decision that should be made by both biological parents, step aside and let the child's parents decide how to handle the situation. Even if you disagree with what they decide or the punishment they put in place, we need to detach from that decision. We parent like we parent and our mate and ex-spouse parent like they parent. Just because a family is merged does not mean that your partner will parent the same way you do. Discussions need to be had so that you are both on the same page. This is critical in making a merged family work.

For example, Nick's principal called John on November 2nd and told him that Nick did not attend school the entire month of October. What to do next was not up to me, even though I shared my opinion (and a bit of laughter – why didn't they call on October 3rd?). And I should not have laughed so hard because I found out that Becca forged my name on notes at least 3 times a week during her senior year so she could get out of school early.

John and I might have had discussions about how to handle, but it was up to John and Nick's mom to decide what punishment, if any, they would enforce. Whether I agree or disagree, it was up to me to accept what they decide.

<u>When One has a Child and the Other Does Not.</u>

Merging families can also be difficult when one person has children and the other does not. It can be eye opening for a single person to adapt to a life with a partner who has children. When you have children, you know they might go bonkers because they haven't had their nap or they are hungry. It's frustrating to a parent, but it is a behavior you get used to when you are with them day in and day out. When you are single, you only need to be concerned about yourself, then when you date, it's just you and your partner. Add in a few kids every other weekend and it might be a bit overwhelming. Just know what you are getting into and spend quality time with the children so you can build a healthy bond with them. Have patience and soon they will grow out of this stage and onto another! It is important to know whether this is something you will commit to, because if you marry, your new family will include your mate and his children.

So, what happens if your children do not accept your new partner? John and I discussed this quite a bit. Let's say Becca did not want John around and she ignored him when he came over. John was always nice to her and was interested in hearing about her friends and school. Each time he talked to her, she was standoffish and not nice. In this scenario if her aloofness continued, I would have an honest talk with her and find out what was bothering her about John. I witnessed the interactions and knew he was sincere and trying. Eventually she admitted that she was afraid that I wouldn't spend any time with her. As a parent, I assured her that I love her more than life itself and I'd always be there for her. Always.

But what if the child never comes around. It could be a teenager going through a tough stage and takes anger out on the one you are dating. If there is no justification that your partner mistreated your child, communication is key. The child or teenager might not want you to date for several reasons. They expect you and your ex to get back together. They feel bad their ex is not dating anyone and you have moved on. They would feel guilty if they developed a relationship with you. Open communication is key. Talk with your child and encourage your partner and child to take steps to build a rapport with each other.

Set Same Rules For all. No favorites.

When you become a family unit, it's important to set the same rules for all, obviously taking age into consideration. Coming together is a transition for all because everyone is different. As parents and step parents, we need to be mindful of being fair and equal.

Tell the kids upfront what behaviors you will not allow. We would set a timer when they fought about using the computer or PlayStation. No name calling was allowed. If we had to separate them into different

181

rooms, we did that. Most important was to have the same deal for all the kids. It showed fairness and that all were treated in the same manner. I believe this created safety and consistency for each child.

Be adventurous as a family.

Every other weekend, Nick, Becca and Dan stayed with me and John. At least one day we would do something fun as a family. Whether it be going on a hike, fishing, a theatre, roller skating, tubing, the movies, laser tag, paint ball, ice skating, skiing, ziplining or anything to get them out of the house and experience new things.

There is a small theatre company in the next town and each year I'd be sure to purchase tickets to A Christmas Carol. One time we got lucky and sat in the front row. Well, Dan didn't think so, because the ghost from Christmas past tended to spit while he read his lines, and the spit landed on Dan's face. From then on, the closest we sat was the 5th row. Spit generally doesn't travel that far in the 5th row.

Simple. Don't demean your ex in front of the kids.

Even though we don't want to admit it, after a split there are two sides. Each person made mistakes.

We may still get resentful and bitter about something our ex did or does, but for the kids' sake, we need to refrain from saying negative comments in front of the children. Remember that your ex is their mommy or daddy. Like it or not, we will always have the ex in our lives and any negative thing you say about the parent can cut deep and be very hurtful. If you are upset with your ex, talk to your spouse or vent to a friend, but refrain from putting him down in front of the children.

I was in a department store recently and there were two young kids being pushed in a carriage by the dad, who was f-bombing their mother, calling her names and insulting her. I intentionally walked down their aisle to shut him up. I saw fear in the eyes of those children. The woman turned around. I mouthed to her, "Are you okay?" She said yes and walked by me.

Seeing those little boys faces when he was hurting their mom was heartbreaking. Count to ten before you speak ill of your ex.

Find common ground with each child.

Each child will have his or her own personality, likes, dislikes, food favorites, hobbies, temperament. It is up to the step-parent to get to know the child and to find common interests. You will bond with each kid in a different way.

Sometimes you might struggle with finding similar things you both like to do, so develop some. Take an interest in what she/he likes and try it yourself.

Always remember that you are the adult and the kids did not ask for this situation. They are going through this transition the same as other family members. But they are children and may not have the tools to deal. Even if your step children are older, try to have an experience you both can enjoy.

Building solid relationships take time. You might not be a biological parent, but you can be adult role model in their lives and create a wonderful bond with your step children, regardless of age.

Stepping Out In Love

Part 4

EVERYDAY LIFE

BUTT OUT

There is no worse nag than a young child. Not even a disgruntled wife can hold a candle to a kid who wants something. Becca did not like my smoking habit. I started smoking cigarettes just prior to the divorce. I have an addictive personality and one cigarette led to a pack a day habit…almost as soon as I took my first puff. Becca was 5 and pestered me daily to quit smoking.

I knew this pint-sized squirt was right, but I was not ready to quit. I liked to smoke. Every time the topic of quitting came up, a million valid reasons popped up as to why I should keep doing it. It calms me, it's better than shooting heroin, it's not that bad for me, it helps keep weight off.

Then one day I put my stubbornness aside and thought, "Well, when will I stop?" I mean I do want to quit at some point and I would have to pick a day. Then I thought (after a disgusting, gagging, coughing spell) what happens if I get lung cancer and leave my young girl motherless?

The thought of something that dreadful happening made me finally act. I knew the side effects of quitting were going to be brutal, as I had quit in my early twenties. The withdrawals, the intense cravings, the night sweats when all the toxins leave my body, missing my daily smokes. What was I going to do with my hands on the drive to work? Enduring all this stuff was going to be tough and I was very aware of how torturous it was going to be. But if I did not quit, and I got sick, *then the consequence of getting sick would be way more brutal than quitting cold turkey.*

I made the decision and finally quit. May 7, 2001. It was not easy. I was grumpy and irritable. I gained weight. Every time I saw an active smokestack on the highway, it reminded me of a cigarette and I had an
186

anxiety attack. I missed the cig during the drive to work and the butt during work lunch when I would hide behind a flower bush, so no one would

discover my habit. I missed the butts while out drinking with friends. I missed the physical handling of a cigarette and my mouth missed it too. I missed watching the smoke come out of my mouth and blowing cool smoke rings. I lost my consoler and soother. I missed my stinky, tooth-staining habit.

I have heard the withdrawal of nicotine is just as intense as coming off heroin. I can't say for sure because I have not tried heroin, but if heroin withdrawal is anything like nicotine withdrawal, I feel badly for them.

I did this for Becca, for me, my finances, my lungs and a healthier future. This was another layer of the onion that needed peeling. Giving up smoking to me was probably the hardest thing I've ever done; worse than a c-section, a colonoscopy, exercising, worse than having a root canal.

I am thankful every day that I quit. And if I can do it, anyone can!

EXTENSIONS

Let's face it, when you marry someone, you technically marry their family also. You'll have to put more place settings at the table during holidays, birthdays and special occasions. The parties you throw could probably double in size. It is critical to form solid relationships. I was the first daughter-in-law in my ex's family and his mother morphed into the mother I had always yearned for. She is the answer to years of prayer. I told my ex, I'm divorcing you, not your family. Even today, my mother-in-law and I complete each other's sentences. Leah is loving, generous, compassionate, endearing and the best mother who never had to give birth to me!

I grew up with a step-mother and step-brother, so extended families are not a new concept for me. After a while, they become family. No need for labels. You spend a lot of time together and even though they are not blood, they are family.

My sister's ex-husband has been so good to me. I have such a fondness for him. He's always been kind and supportive. Laughs, games, cookouts, holidays and treating me like his own kid sister. And I feel the same.

I basically grew up with my ex's family. His brothers and their awesome wives. We were three young, married couples who bonded, goofed around and got along wonderfully. It was easy. As we each started having children, our bonds grew even tighter. Our kids are close in age and in heart. Even though we divorced and don't see each other often, the strong connection we built years ago returns instantly when we see each other.

I immediately connected with each member of John's family. They graciously welcomed me with open arms. We enjoy special vacations, dinners, holidays and most recently my nephew's fairytale wedding. Oh what a night! So many special events to look forward to!

Even though they are not technically my blood brothers and sisters in law anymore, my life has been enhanced by each and every bond I have been fortunate enough to marry into!!

THE GALS

If someone told young Gayle, who was ridiculed every day of her adolescent existence, that she would be surrounded by a plethora of amazing friends, I would have made the pffff sound and rolled my eyes in the back of my head.

What is it that connects us more to one person than another? Why is it that we can instantly bond with someone after getting to know them for 5 minutes, but don't have that connection with someone we've known our entire life?

Ah girlfriends. You meet, click and bond. Could have been in your neighborhood, high school, college, or work and you have this undeniable connection.

I have a group of seven female friends that I met in high school and college. Some of the most incredible moments of my life have been with these women. One day while on Cape Cod we decided to crash a million-dollar open house. I was first through the door and the rest of the crazy eights followed. The broker met us as we came through the door.

"Hi I'm Gayle!" I gestured behind me and introduced the girls. "And these are my sister wives." His jaw dropped as he watched my girls enter his 6-figure listing. We goof and we laugh. It's what we do.

There are so many layers of friendships. Sometimes I crave a friend who:

- I can talk about God with. Someone who knows the fundamental principles of the Bible and we can dig deep about the meaning of life and what our purpose is. I am invigorated talking with a friend who is a bright light in this often-dark world. The friend who is positive and compassionate and lives a life I want to emulate. She is my role model and mentor.

- Brings out my insanely goofy side. The friend who allows me to completely let my guard down, cracks up at my disgusting and inappropriate stories, and makes me laugh until I can't breathe.

- I can vent to. The one who will let me vent for hours, will not try to solve my problems, but will nod and understand. She will stroke my hair, wipe my tears and hand me as many Puff Puffs as needed.

- Wants to party like it's 1999. In my younger years, I was quite the party girl extraordinaire. Can't remember those days, but I remember having a blast. Best days when we were carefree and had the whole world in front of us!

- I haven't seen in a long while and yearn to be with her again. Sitting down at dinner, hours feeling like minutes and amazing how easy it is to reconnect and reminisce.

- Has better fashion sense than I do. She'll help me pick out an outfit with pretty accessories and matching lipstick that I'll never wear.

- Is okay with being quiet. No words. Just girlfriends in the same room in stillness.

- Likes to eat. Go big or go home. Get the gooey hot fudge sundae after boxing up half our meal.

- Talk about the latest book club recommendations and Netflix new releases.

- Have a heartfelt conversation with the friend who understands what it was like growing up in a dysfunctional home, who struggles with food and weight, is super-duper strong and independent.

Most of my friends have been in my life for a very long time. I joke as we get older saying that I think I need to get younger friends. These gals have seen me at my finest, worst, drunkest, laziest, shrewdest, goofiest, wisest, whiniest, stubbornest, stupidest, brattiest. And you know what? They are still here with me. I might not see everyone all the time, but when I think of them I feel a warmth in my heart, and the realness of our bond.

I think back to memories of that Nor'easter in college when we did snow angels at 2 am; the countless times that people overheard us cracking up in a restaurant and asked to pull up a chair to join us; the sex assignments we gave each other (Our husbands couldn't wait for us to come home to find out what homework we received); my dorm neighbor feeding me goldfish when I stumbled home from a party; the laughter we share when I perform my impression of the talking dog – 'Yeh? Cover it with what?'; the completely inappropriate conversations we have when we just let loose; the fight for the front seat; wondering how one friend will explain to the other that during her vacation, her brand new clothes with the tags still on ended up on the floor in her closet covered in cat urine; pinky swearing that we will remove any chin hairs we might have while lying in our coffin; going to plays, concerts, new restaurants and clubs; pays me the highest compliment by spitting out her drink when I say something funny; flash-dancing over Phyllis' porta-potty; sleeping over my friend's house after going to a Chippendales show and the last thing she said before we went to sleep is, "I'm going to be dreaming about butts all night."

I am at my best when surrounded by the friends that I love and who love me. It is a sense of security and acceptance that only friendship can bring.

These women are priceless. You can't buy any of these memories with a Mastercard. I choose to water and nourish our relationships till the end of time.

Luv joos!

IN SICKNESS AND IN...DID YOU PASS?

Life throws all kinds of situations at us. Just because we find our soul mate doesn't mean that life is all gum drops and unicorns. Life is life and things happen. We deal with minor illnesses and sometimes an illness that will blow your socks off.

On June 5th, 2009 I had a stomach ache.

This tummy ache escalated from a few uncomfortable cramps to vomiting and excruciating pain.

Laying down behind the curtain in the ER, IV drugs wiped away my pain the second they entered my bloodstream. The ER resident, Doogie Howzer, said my blood work indicated I had a nasty infection and my red, white and blue blood cell count was 8 billion. (Flying high on Dilaudid at this point...) I remember being wheeled into surgery to remove a growth on my intestines. It was called Meckel's Diverticulum, a condition most commonly diagnosed in infants. I was born with this growth and at age 45 it decided to make a dramatic, painful appearance. Angry and ready to burst, the surgeon told me if it exploded, I would have exploded too.

After the surgery, I was put on a morphine drip and began to hallucinate. At night, the leaves on my curtain would turn into robots and bunnies. They would jump off the curtain and set up a picnic at the foot of my bed. They kept me company at night.

Along with hanging out with imaginary creatures in the dark, the morphine apparently removed my mouth filter. John's birthday happened to be the day of my surgery, and I had a special treat planned for him in the boudoir. I guess while in recovery I told the nurses about

194

his "special treat" and how badly I felt that he did not receive it. When I'm in my right state of mind I overshare, so you can imagine the detail I went into while on a heavy dose of narcotics. I had them in hysterics and won the title of their favorite patient! John later asked me why all the nurses stared at him when he walked by.

To save my marriage and John's dignity, I requested to have my pain meds changed. No more stories or bunny visits.

After intestinal surgery, the doctors cannot release a patient until all internal organs are functioning properly. Since I was hospitalized for 11 days, I was repeatedly asked, "Hi Gayle. Have you passed gas today?" No one asked if I enjoyed my breakfast or if I would like a more fashionable pair of hospital socks. Oh no. The only thing they had on their filthy minds was whether or not I tooted. And I swear the hospital went to the Chippendales mall and intentionally handpicked hot interns to mortify me on purpose. After a while I smartened up and before anyone who walked in my room got anywhere near my bed, I put my hand up and said "Don't Even Ask. The answer is NO! Off you go! Shoo!"

I do have my pride you know.

I had at least five subsequent hospital stays after my initial surgery, all due to scar tissue blockages. For three of those admissions, they put a stupid NG tube put up my nose and down to my belly. All administered stone cold sober. For anyone who has had this experience, you know how torturous this procedure is. I have given birth, had shingles, had a tooth pulled without Novocain and nothing, I mean nothing, compared to this pain.

During the last day of my hospital stay, I had just begun the process of introducing solid foods. With blockages, they starve you for the first two days, then onto a light mushy diet. After eating a bit of delightful squishy food, I went to the restroom. I turned to flush and glanced down to a bowl full of blood. I panicked and immediately pushed my call button. Like five times. I sat on the edge of the bed and cried. Was I dying? Is this internal bleeding? The nurse rushed into my bathroom and examined the contents of the bowl. She called for another nurse's opinion. Then one more nurse rushed into my bathroom. The three medical professionals were chatting back and forth, each bent over with their faces 2 inches from my red pee.

Turning to me, Nurse 1 asked, "Honey, what did you eat today?"

"I had 4 Jell-O's."

"Oh honey, that's strawberry Jell-O in the bowl, not blood. See there? That's a Jell-O swirl!"

We all laughed and snorted until we cried. This time, happy tears.

A few years later John came back from a routine dental cleaning and his hygienist felt a lump in his neck. She recommended he get it checked out.

John came home after the biopsy results and yes, it was thyroid cancer. He informed me in the same manner as if was telling me he paid the electric bill. Monotone, flat and dry. Sometimes I wonder if he has a pulse.

John had cancer. Such a surreal thing to comprehend. Thyroid cancer has a very high recovery rate, but he did have to have surgery to remove the tumor, so there was risk involved. John did not appear phased at all. He just didn't show fear. Or emotion of any kind.

On the morning of his operation, the surgeon told us it would be a two-hour surgery. I made sure my phone charger was with me in the waiting area so I could play Candy Crush uninterrupted. I didn't see any raffles going on. Bummer. Six hours later I'm still sitting there with no lives left and I'm freaking out a bit. Why the heck is it taking so long? There obviously were risks, but he assured us it would be a relatively routine surgery. Finally, the surgeon came out and told me I could see him. Guess the tumor was near the vocal chords and in a tough spot to remove.

John was loopy as expected but felt okay once the anesthesia wore off. He was discharged and the incision across his neck was recovering nicely after a few days. The only issue he had was that his voice did not return. He could only speak in a loud whisper, at best. You basically had to sit on top of him to hear what he was saying. Poor guy. He never complained. Well, I take that back. He did complain when I was at the top of the stairs yelling out a question and I couldn't hear him answer. I kept forgetting he didn't have a voice!

His coworkers called him the Godfather when he spoke on conference calls. We all had some laughs at his expense. That's how we roll.

I frequently made him eggs because he had cancer. He would look at me with his puppy, sad, pathetic eyes and ask, "Can you make me some eggs? I have cancer." What was I supposed to do, say NO?

John's voice did return to normal after about 6 months.

Being married is not all fun and cupcakes. It's about Jell-O and cancer and eggs and jokes and NG tubes and gratitude.

TORTURE, SUFFERING, AGONY…I MEAN CAMPING

John enjoys camping so against my better judgment, we went with the kids as a bonding experience before we were married.

As the five of us pulled out of the driveway in our mini-van, the only thing that wasn't packed was my bedroom dresser. Literally, we were transporting the entire house. John bought a tent, so we were camping old school. We found our barren site which was surrounded by expandable, custom designed 60-foot trailers.

John and I retrieved the 4,000 pipes and poles from the trunk. We knew the kids, ages 7, 8, and 9 would not be much help so we told them to look around. This campground was on a beautiful lake and had a heated pool, mini golf course, fishing docks, boat ramps, volleyball net, big field to play sports and a beautiful mountain behind us, so there was a lot for them to explore. We gave Nick a walkie talkie and told both Nick and Becca not to go too far off and to stay together. In other words, don't lose Dan. Off they went, and John and I began assembling our nylon house.

About a half hour later, just as I finished blowing up our bedroom set, Nick and Becca came strolling back.

"Where's Dan?" John questioned.

Both kids shrugged and said, "We were walking up the mountain and Dan went the other way when we got to the top."

"WHAT?" John was beside himself. Rightly so, it was less than an hour and we already lost a kid.

"Go back up there and retrace where you went and *FIND HIM!*" John's veins don't usually bulge but they were poppin'.

A few minutes after Nick and Becca left to look for Dan, a man driving a golf cart (we later found out he was the campground cop) drove up to our site. Dan was sitting beside him. Poor little thing. He had been found! We let Becca and Nick sweat it out for a while and didn't immediately walkie talkie them that he was safe and found.

After the rescue, my biggest rule after "Don't lose Dan," was no dirty feet in the tent house. The five of us were sharing a two-room tent and I did not want worms or crud on the floor. We had a small tent mud room so they could easily wipe off their feet before stepping into the bedroom.

Shortly after Nick and Becca returned, it started to rain. John and I sat on our air mattress bed waiting for it to pass. 4 hours later it was still raining. The kids played board games and cards by lantern.

Eventually we went to sleep. There was nothing else to do. We had fancy window things and they were left slightly unzipped during the rain, so my sleeping bag was soggy. The kids were giggling on the other side of the tent. All three kids on one air mattress, Becca sleeping on the outside edge. John was happy as a clam. Not sure if he was on drugs, because anyone in that situation had to be high.

I lied still in the damp sleeping bag on the lumpy air bed and stared above as bugs and spiders walked across the canvas roof. The shadows cast from the outside light made them appear to be human sized. I listened to the thunder and it kept me up most of the night. After a while, I started sweating and wanted to adjust my leg so it was out of the sleeping bag, but I was paralyzed at the thought that a creature would slide in with me if I unzipped anything.

We woke up the next morning to more rain. Becca had slept in a puddle of mud after being accidentally pushed off the air mattress. She was crabby and tired. I was miserable, didn't sleep, was soggy and sweaty and started complaining. It was 8:15 am. Around 8:30 am, our friends came for a visit and brought us donuts and hot drinks! I was so happy to see them! I asked if I could sneak home with them.

As they drove away, a lonely tear fell down my face.

I turned back with my head held low toward our temporary housing. I cleaned off my dirty feet and wiggled back into my air bed and closed my eyes. It was 9:10 am.

The kids were tired of playing cards and decided to play outside in the rain. I was despondent at this point and mumbled. "Have yourself a ball." They skipped off into the down pouring abyss.

I found my secret goodie stash and felt a sense of relief as I sucked down a bag of chips and a chocolate bar. A few hours later after waking up from my nap, I went out to look for the kids. They were heading back to our campsite. Literally frozen, I watched as our precious children jumped from puddle to puddle, covered head to toe in mud.

Nine hours after we set up our home away from home I looked at John with my best puppy dog eyed impression.

I asked the only question that made sense.

"Can we go home now?" I whined.

He reluctantly agreed. As fast as humanly possible, we showered, shoved all the wet poles, string, canvas and sleeping bags in the car, drove home, ordered a pizza and watched a movie in the comfort of our own home. Best movie ever!

Stepping Out In Love

361 days later…

The mini-van is packed, this time with fishing poles and wiggly night crawlers. I agreed to go again because 1) we were renting a camper (for more money than a five-star hotel); 2) we were on the lake with a private dock; 3) I brought vodka; and 4) because the kids nagged me until I caved. Quite persistent little squirts.

When we arrived at the entrance gate, we were given keys to camper #95. I ordered the deluxe special which included a kids' package with t-shirts, mugs, chocolate, crackers and marshmallows and small games for the kids. This is camping done right!

The camper looked like a mansion to me. The door was ajar and we all were quite impressed with our weekend digs. The kids immediately made bed assignments. We unpacked the entire car: the food, pillows, sleeping bags, clothes, fishing poles, games, bathing suits, coolers, towels, water bottles, paper towels, condiments, snacks, blankets, wood, lanterns, toiletries etc.

I looked all over the camper and could not locate the deluxe kids' package. Once all was settled I called the office and asked about it.

The young woman on the phone seemed confused and said. "It should be on the counter."

"Nope, it's not here. I don't see it anywhere."

She apologized and said she'll walk it down to us in a few minutes.

"Thank you so much!"

It was a beautiful day. The sky was Easter-egg-blue. There was a gentle breeze and the lake was beautiful. We were secluded enough to have a decent amount of privacy. I was pleased to know that tonight my head would be on a pillow and not in mud.

Meanwhile, the kids were getting their fishing gear together and John and I were building a fire. As our adorable fishermen walked down to the dock, a car pulled up right behind our van. A man got out was looking back and forth at our camper and at our neighbor's camper. He asked what number we were staying in and we said #95. He thought our camper was his camper but was not sure because the site number on the tree was in between the two sites.

Since the door was ajar, we did not try our keys in the lock. I went over to our empty neighbor camper and holy freaking voila, our key fit perfectly. I walked inside and lo and behold there was a huge gift basket on the counter. Oh crap! As I left the cabin, a young camp employee was walking toward us with an identical, huge gift basket. I embarrassingly explained what happened and she told me to keep both baskets. I'm sure she mumbled to herself, "Camper loser".

John and I moved everything to the other camper. Seriously – it's still Friday? We had to make sure the kids knew where we were living now.

The rest of the weekend was bearable. I'm done with camping. I've sacrificed enough.

Thirteen years later…

"Hon, I used to go to Mongaup pond camping when I was a teen. It's on a lake and so beautiful. I will reserve a perfect spot right on the water and you will love it." John was pleading with me.

"Nah, sounds nice, but I'll pass."

"C'mon, I had cancer."

The cancer card again. Seriously?

202

Stepping Out In Love

"Okay I'll go." waaaaaaaaa

"I will buy a new tent, one with two rooms. It'll be awesome!!" He was like a kid on Christmas. I was like a woman descending the stairway to hell.

The things we do for our beloveds. And cancer.

We arrived at the site and granted, it was a perfect spot. It was mid-June and the weather was ideal. Once again, we unpacked the whole damn van and set up our nylon and mesh house. I was older now and had little patience for bugs and dirt. Once you hit a certain point in life, it's hard to sleep with bugs.

As John was setting up the lanterns and gas stove, I made sandwiches for dinner. We assembled a separate screen house so critters would not get into the food. I took out the mayonnaise, turkey and bread and made a sandwich. As I turned my back for 2 seconds to grab the macaroni salad, a massive daddy long legs crawled on my Wonder bread. John was heating up a pouch of freeze-dried Alpo-looking vomit for his dinner.

It was dark after we finished eating and it was time for a potty run. We were about a half mile away from the bathrooms. I grabbed a flashlight and noticed a path that looked like a shortcut. Although the path was shorter, it also contained a huge clump of spider webs. As I walked directly into the giant web, I screamed, shimmied and shook and wriggled and screamed again. This cannot be happening. I envisioned moths, gnats, black bugs and beetles smushed all over me. I had chills at the thought of removing the dead critters and webbing from my hair. My hair! My beautiful hair now filled with creepy, flying crawlies!

I went to the bathroom and pre-menopausal me who never knows when her "friend" would pay a visit, paid a visit. Are you f-ing kidding me? Luckily, I am always prepared. Unluckily, I once read that bears sense when the "friend" is nearby.

While I was still in the stall I heard some loud pinging on the building. Now what? Was someone throwing rocks at me? No. That would have been too reasonable. It was hailing. Hail the size of nickels. I was a half mile away from the tent, didn't have an umbrella or hail hat, had a head full of dead bugs, just got my period and am now bear bait.

I bolted back to the tent, this time consciously avoiding the short cut, and jumped in my sleeping bag, soaking wet. I attempted to sleep and may have dozed off here and there, but my back started to ache, my stomach was crampy and every three minutes or so I unzipped the window to see if Baloo was trying to locate his supper. I woke up the next morning, which was a positive sign, yet my back was killing me. It felt like I slept on a rock. Apparently, I did sleep on a rock because our air mattress had a leak in it.

I was beyond miserable and poor John knew it. I couldn't hold back my words. I wanted to stomp and throw myself on the ground. I wanted my own bed that doesn't deflate! I wanted clean hair! I didn't want to be dinner!

Once I had my fit and settled down, John and I sat near the fire. It was a nice moment between us. At one point I heard him say, "Honey, I love you."

I looked over at him and thought He is so sweet! He's trying to make the best of this miserable experience. I replied, "I love you too honey!" I hated camping, but I loved him.

He said, "I love you too honey, but I actually said, "'Honey, you have a bug on you."

"That's it. I'm done."

Never again. I sat in the car and we went home.

FAMILY LAUGHS

Best Times Ever.

- When Becca was 16 and learning to drive, we had our share of battles. I tried to calm myself prior to each driving lesson, but quickly became frazzled when I feared my head would go through the nearest mailbox. She and I hit a rough patch and I thought a game night would help turn her into a more pleasant teen...and a better driver. At one point during Pictionary, I looked over at her and she had the biggest smile on her face, along with orange Dorito stains. I knew game night was the right move!

- In the summer, we'd build a bonfire out in the backyard and make smores. One memorable night shortly before Nick left for army basic training and Becca for college, John, the kids and I sat around the fire. John started telling stories of when the boys were born, how gross witnessing childbirth was, and the crazy things they did as little boys. John should do stand up. This bit was hysterical.

- After a family campfire, John and I went in the house and the kids remained by the fire alone. About an hour later I heard singing, and although it was dark, I saw someone running around the backyard. I smiled and went to bed. Next day I asked Becca what on earth they were doing.

  She said, "We were playing Truth or Dare. Dan dared Nick to lick the cat's head. Nick dared Dan to lick the cat's head in the same spot. I dared Dan to pull his underwear up and stick his arms out through the sides. I ran around the volleyball net screaming, "I believe I can fly!" while flapping my arms like a bird. Nick dared Dan to stand in the middle of the driveway and sing the national anthem. I was dared to lick someone's elbow." Pure, unadulterated fun!

- Nick was in 1st grade and he got in trouble. His principal gave Nick a note for his parents to sign. Nick was to return the signed note to the principal the next day. The principal called Nick's mom and dad into his office and showed them the note. Nick forged his mother's name on the note and the 'e' in her name was backwards. They tried to hold back and not crack up.

- I picked up Becca from a 7th grade dance and asked how her night was. She burst out laughing and told me how the police officer on duty told her and her friends (girlfriends) to stop grinding. It was the only incident of the night. She thought she was so cool.

- Finding out the kids figured out our parental pin number when they were 10 years old. All those years they were watching R rated movies. Oops. They told us when they were in their 20's.

- Nick and Dan were heading into Best Buy and right before we walked through the entrance, this gigantic bird flew above us and dropped a huge poop on my cheek. Immediately both kids leaned over and cracked up. I was paralyzed, grossed out, screaming and yelling for someone to GET IT OFF ME! They just laughed and laughed until no sound came out.

- Nick is 6'5", Dan is 6'2" and Becca is 5'1". When standing, the top of Becca's head just reaches Nick's belly button. Since Becca is so short, Nick and I saw a person driving in front of us that looked like no one was driving because we couldn't see a head. Nick smiled and pointed to the car ahead of us, "There's Becca!"

- Since Nick and Dan are so tall, heads always turn when we walk through a restaurant. One day before going to TGI Fridays, Nick had just returned from boot camp training and had bloody gashes all over his face and arms. Dan went rock climbing that day and a branch snapped in his face. Both had bloody faces, arms and looked like they just came from a barroom brawl. I still remember everyone looked at us trying to figure out what on earth happened to those big boys!

- Because Nick was always tall, people always thought he was older than his actual age. When he was at a town pool, a 15-year old girl started up a conversation with him. She asked him what he liked to do. He innocently replied, "I like to play with army guys." He was 9. She left.

- When John had thyroid cancer, we handled it differently than most couples. Statistics showed that thyroid cancer has a high cure rate, so we were optimistic that after his surgery he would be fine. He came out fine except he lost his voice for a few months. At Becca's graduation my friend brought my dad and John flowers – both for enduring cancer. John said as he looked at the fragrant purple bundle, "Now this made having cancer worth it."

- Being his supportive girlfriend, I drove John to his physician's office while he was getting snipped...I mean fixed. While waiting in the visitor's area, I noticed there was a raffle going on down the hall. I bought a few tickets and an hour later they called out my name! I won this massive gift basket full of teas, coffee, chocolates and biscuits! I was so happy! Who knew that I'd have such luck on V Day! A while later, John comes out of the office walking slowly and awkwardly. I immediately got up and exclaimed, "Look what I won honey!!"

He replied, "Oh, how nice. I'm in there watching the smoke lift off my balls and you're winning prizes."

THE HONEYMOON IS OVER

When your relationship progresses and it's heading toward a serious commitment, it's like playing house. Everything is new and fresh, you canoodle like rabbits, go away every weekend, eat out frequently, life is like a fairy tale.

Over time you settle into a routine and become more relaxed with each other. Walking around with no makeup on wearing sweatpants, hair sticking up in a million directions. Now I'm at the point where I don't even wear pants half the time!

Occasionally, a situation occurs that confirms the honeymoon is over with absolute certainty. Here are a few examples.

I woke up one morning and John was visibly upset.

"What's wrong honey?" I asked.

With his head hung low, he sheepishly said, "I think I might have pooped in my pants during the night. It's weird but it was on the *outside* of my underwear."

Curious, I sat up and said, "What are you talking about? Can I see your underwear?"

He leaned over the laundry basket and grabbed the top pair of undies and tossed them to me. Yep, there was the stain.

To John's horror, I put the white fabric up to my nose and sniffed. "Oh honey, you didn't poop in your pants!! This is my missing Hershey drop that fell in the bed last night! I looked everywhere for it. I'm glad you found it!"

+++

It feels special when I notice John smile lovingly at me from across the room. It's so endearing and makes me feel like I'm the only girl in the world!

One morning during a winter storm, I woke up and John had a big smile on his face as he was staring at me. He probably was counting his blessings at how lucky he was to be my husband.

I turned and looked lovingly back at him, then laid my head back on the pillow and asked, "What are you thinking about? How much you love me?"

He laughed and replied, "With you lying there like that, the steam coming from the humidifier behind you looks like it's coming out of your nose, like a dragon." He cracked up.

I punched him in the arm.

+++

Most nights I fall asleep before John. Generally, once my head hits the pillow I'm out. John takes a while to fall asleep. He usually reads for a while, then watches a boring science show and finally drifts off.

We watched a crime series one night. When we went to bed, I quickly fell asleep, as usual. About an hour later, I was awakened by a loud bang! It sounded like a gunshot. "John! OMG, did you hear that? Was that a gunshot? Is someone in the house? Did you hear that – it woke me out of a sound sleep!!!" My heart was pounding out of my chest.

Yet John didn't even look my way. He dryly said, "No Gayle, you farted."

Yes, my dear friends, the honeymoon is over.

210

TUESDAYS WITH NORMIE

Daddy passed away last year. It is still extremely difficult to wrap my head around the fact that I will never see him again. I will never be able to look into his deep blue eyes, watch his beaming smile light up a room or soak up every word of his wise advice.

He was sick with lung cancer for several years. Witnessing the ups and downs of that disease is brutal. In the last five years of his life, he had a heart valve replacement, a lung removed, chemo and radiation, and countless doctor appointments and ER visits. All endured with a huge grin, twinkly eyes, an optimistic attitude and strong faith of beating this atrocious disease. For me, his youngest daughter, a piece of me chipped away each time we parted, praying that time was not the last time we would spend together.

This adorable man was my Daddy. He was not 'Father' or even 'Dad', he was Daddy. He had a devoted, strong, committed, quiet love for his girls.

As a young 16-year old born and raised in Canada, he moved to Florida, spoke very little English, was first in his high school to buy an ultra-cool Austen Healey car, built a tremendously successful contracting business, bought a huge chunk of land the year I was born, retired at age 45 after selling the land and helped as many people as he possibly could during his entire lifetime.

When my parents divorced, I was 14, my sister married shortly afterward, and Daddy and I lived on our own. At that time, it was relatively unheard of for the father to be granted legal custody of his children, but Daddy fought for us. It was a no brainer for me to choose to live with him.

He met his wife Toni when I was 16 and they were together over 30 years. He would frequently tell me how much he appreciated her and that their time together made him so happy. She took very good care of him. They had a nice balance where she had her hobbies, he had his, and they also did things together.

Daddy taught me to do all things with excellence and integrity. Anyone who witnessed my father's homemade breakfasts or stepped on his velvety green lawn knew that his work product was flawless. Whether it be perfectly straight bacon strips or minuscule details in the home he built, everything was done with perfection. If there was an error, he would rip it apart and start over from scratch and complete it the proper way. Anyone who was the recipient of his work product, knew that they would get outstanding quality.

Daddy was a shrewd businessman. He would not enter into any shady agreements or compromise his business at any cost. He was a man of his word and followed through on his commitments. He could be tough as nails and drive a hard bargain. I have seen him in action negotiating and understood why he was successful. I watched him pick his battles and let some things go, but when an issue was crucial, he stood firm in his convictions and didn't back down. I happen to be the same way.

Daddy showed me that you can merge a stepfamily and love your partner's child as much as you love your own children. My father respected and loved my stepbrother Anthony. They had a close bond and Daddy knew he could rely on Anthony when he needed him. This taught me so much about love when I merged my own stepfamily. Just because the kids were not my biological kids, didn't mean I couldn't love and care about them with all my heart, and treat them as if they were my own.

Daddy rarely said a bad word about anyone. He did not judge others. Even as a general contractor for so many years, he understood people made mistakes and was forgiving, yet he did not allow them to repeat the same mistakes on him. He was wise and discerning but not judgmental. Those are incredible and rare qualities.

Everyone loved my father. Chris and I threw him a surprise 80th birthday party. Best decision ever. Over 100 family and friends attended "the party of his life," as he referred to it. I will never forget when he walked into the fake 'graduation' party and everyone sang Happy Birthday to him, he looked over and asked, "For me?" His smile was infectious and huge. He was quite a character who was adored by many.

At some point in my 40's Daddy decided not to exchange birthday gifts with me and Chris. I said that was fine, but he had to pick out a card for our birthdays. I specifically said I didn't want anyone to pick it out for him, *he* had to pick it out. He agreed and over the years I have received some of the most beautiful and heartfelt cards that Hallmark had ever written. Daddy was a man of few words when it came to expressing his inner emotions, but boy, his feelings came out in those amazing cards. Some may have had 10 words on them, but I know that card reflected his thoughts. Sometimes, he told me, he would go to three different stores to find just the right card for us. I could have told him it would have been easier to pick up an Amazon gift card, but no sweater on earth could compare to the priceless pre-written words on those cards, so I kept my mouth shut. And I kept every single one of those cards.

For many years prior to his death, I met Daddy on Tuesdays for dinner. Otherwise known as Tuesdays with Normie. We had our special table in the back and each week we would talk about everything and anything. My sister and step brother would also come. Daddy was so pleased that we were together during these dinners. I know he loved us and was proud of each one of us.

During his last days, Daddy was home surrounded by friends and family. On the Saturday before he passed, there was a line of visitors who came to the house to say goodbye. He was alert and still had a sense of humor. I think this showing of love gave him an adrenaline burst because he was enjoying every moment, smiling when loved ones sat by his bedside. I knew he was pleased that so many took the time to be with him.

Even though it was emotional, it was important for me to witness this outpouring of love. Watching his best friend Ronnie stand by his side during Daddy's illness, in addition to dealing with his own illness, taught me so much about loyalty and true friendship. As hard as it was for me to lose my father, losing a best friend and loyal confidante is just as devastating. My appreciation for Ronnie runs deep as I know how much my father treasured their bond.

One everyone left, later that night Daddy shared with sadness that he just couldn't beat it. It dawned on me in that vulnerable moment that he was not immortal. I had no words, I just held his hand.

On Sunday, a few more of his 80-something year-old male friends stood over his bed to say goodbye. He was unconscious at this point so he wasn't aware of the tears dropping onto his bed. That encounter was heartbreaking to watch.

He died on a Monday with so much love by his side. In that moment, his eyes opened wider than we'd ever seen. I believe that's when he first saw God. Such a beautiful thought.

My incredible father put up a hell of a fight.

I miss him every day. The lessons he taught me about how to be an amazing friend, provider, businesswoman and parent are embedded in my heart forever.

My hope is that he is in heaven, watching the Red Sox in his favorite recliner, petting our dog Mike, laughing with his brothers and sisters, talking shop with my Pepere Al (my mother's father whom he loved) and telling his slightly embellished stories to John Wayne and Elvis.

So many lives were affected by this man. He might have been small in stature, but he was bigger than life. RIP dear Daddy.

IF ONLY LIFE WORKED BACKWARDS

If I knew back then what I know now, I never would have worried or doubted that life would give me exactly what I needed.

I understand more about life as I get older. I have figured out that God will either give me what I pray for or He won't. Not saying I'm happy about it, but I am beginning to see a pattern that the reason He doesn't give me what I want is because it is not the best fit for me and something else will come along. Usually something better.

Fifteen years into my marriage, I still love John more than ever. If I knew during my single post-divorce years that I would have met such a kind, wonderful man, I probably would have appreciated the single life more than I did, instead of worrying constantly that I would never find my partner.

Life is full of lessons. We learn what we need to learn when we need to learn it. If we don't learn it this time, there will be another opportunity to learn the lesson again. A similar situation will rear its ugly head and I will have a choice to do the same thing, or I can choose to respond differently.

I am learning that anytime I am waiting and am annoyed, life is teaching me patience. Anyone who abandons me is teaching me how to stand up on my own two feet and put self-care first. Anything that angers me is teaching me forgiveness and compassion. Anything that has power over me is teaching me how to take my power back. Anything I hate is teaching me unconditional love. Anything I fear is teaching me courage to step out. Anything I can't control is teaching me how to let go.

Although I wish life worked backwards and I knew what the future holds, I am so grateful to have learned that the storms will not last

216

forever. Life will have ups and downs. I have the choice to protect myself and wait in the boat and ride out the storm or jump in the water and enjoy the adventure and then sit back and enjoy the rainbow.

Over the years, I have heard stories about how a simple tree can be a powerful metaphor for living life.

A tree has a trunk, branches, leaves, and buds. Trees can produce flowers, fruit, and beautiful color. When a wind storm comes along, the tree might lose leaves, branches may break off, and if the trunk is not strong enough, it might bend or split in half.

Beneath the tree are roots. The foundation of the tree. The stronger the roots, the stronger the tree. Roots are not visible, yet they are the most important part of the tree. Without firm, deep roots, the tree has no chance of survival.

If we compare our lives to a tree, the roots would be our core. This includes our integrity, honesty, standards of living, principles, decency, morality. Our backbone. If we develop these qualities and try to live by them, our roots will become strong. Sometimes we go through challenges and trials to strengthen our core. Taking the high road when no one else does, refraining from gossip even though we are chomping at the bit to get in the conversation, going to that self-help group alone to get the help we need, congratulating our coworker who received the promotion we worked so hard to get, yet were passed over.

My roots are grounded in faith also. I try my best to stay in integrity and truth, even when I am alone (meaning when no one is watching what I do and how I act). As my faith and roots grow wider, deeper and thicker, I grow stronger and confident that things will be okay. Even though I don't like the storm I am in the middle of, my roots will continue to strengthen.

The trunk of the tree can be compared to our insight, discernment,

217

wisdom, awareness. We become wiser over time by pressing through pitfalls, compromising in relationships, thriving after hardships and digging deep during an illness. Our instincts develop when we trust our gut. Listening to that quiet voice and knowing the right thing to do, rather than follow the crowd. The more we experience and triumph over, the more our trunks will grow and the stronger they become.

Next comes the branches. I look at the branches as if they are pieces of our personality. Our warmth, sense of humor, work ethic, love of animals, tenacity, creativity, etc.

The leaves are beautiful to look at. The tangible things in our life could be compared to leaves. Our jewelry, homes, clothing, trinkets, special treasures, items passed down from generation to generation. Sometimes we might lose our leaves during stressful situations, but other leaves will grow back over time.

Last but not least, trees produce fruit. Luscious, juicy, nourishing fruit. So important. Matthew 7:15-20 New King James Version (NKJV) "You will know them by their fruit." Fruits of the spirit are love, joy, peace, patience, kindness, goodness, faithfulness, gentleness, and self-control. The fruit we produce and show to others is how we treat others and what draws others to us. It is all about being connected and loving one another.

In order to be that wise old tree, to me, that means to walk in love, loving others and myself, going out of my way to be considerate to strangers and friends, give the benefit of the doubt, treat others as I would want to be treated, attempt to look at the best in any given situation, be loyal and faithful to those you care about, tell the truth always, show gentleness and compassion in all conversations, forgive, let go of bitterness and anger and resentment.

If I look back, my storms came for a reason. The waiting served a purpose, my wrong choices directed me to another path. My worrying did not do a bit of good. Zip. Zilch. Nada.

Challenges during my life have helped me grow, forced me out of my comfort zone, stretched my faith, helped me dig deeper, opened my eyes to a better way to live, prayed to forgive and leg go, and become less critical and judgmental.

Storms do not last forever. The sun will come out. Rainbows will appear.

There is hope for a magnificent future.

There is hope for the heartbroken.

Be blessed and hopeful.

You are loved.

"When I stand before God at the end of my life, I would hope that I would not have a single bit of talent left, and could say, 'I used everything you gave me."

\-   Erma Bombeck

Contact

If you need a speaker for your event, private or group coaching or you just want to chat, please contact me. I would love to support you through any challenge you are facing.

My passion is to give hope to those who are hurting. To offer encouraging and supportive words to those who believe that life will never be good again. To empower those who believe they have no voice. I believe you are incredibly special and can create a beautiful fulfilling life.

Gayle Suzanne Coaching Academy
Online classes available to help you through life's obstacles. Take these courses in the privacy of your own home, at the pace you find most comfortable and return to it time and time again. It is a resource you can use your entire life.
https://gaylesuzanne.teachable.com

Website:
Gaylesuzanne.com

Email:
gayle@gaylesuzanne.com

Facebook.com/GayleSuzanne

Twitter@GayleSuzanne

Made in the USA
Columbia, SC
12 November 2018